Praxis Core Math Study Guide

with Mathematics Workbook and Practice Tests

Academic Skills for Educators

(5732)

Teaching Resources Center
Radford University

Praxis Core Math Study Guide: with Mathematics Workbook and Practice Tests Academic Skills for Educators (5732)

ISBN-13: 978-1-949282-05-4

ISBN-10: 1-949282-05-8

For information on bulk discounts, please contact us at: email@examsam.com

Table of Contents

Geometry Problems:

Statistics and Probability Problems:

Praxis Core Practice Math Test 2:

Praxis Core Practice Math Test 3:

Praxis Core Math Test Format

The Praxis Core Mathematics Test contains the following types of questions:

- Number and Quantity – 17 questions
- Algebra and Functions – 17 questions
- Geometry – 11 questions
- Statistics and Probability – 11 questions

There are 56 questions in total on the Praxis Core math exam.

You will take the exam on a computer, unless you have applied for an exemption.

If you take the test on the computer, an on-screen calculator will be provided for you.

You will have 85 minutes to take the Praxis Core Math Test.

Number and quantity questions cover the following skills:

- Positive and negative integers – including how to perform addition, subtraction, multiplication, and division, as well as understanding how to order numbers from highest to lowest or lowest to highest
- Mathematical equivalents and representing a value in more than one way – for example, converting a fraction to a decimal or percentage
- Whole numbers and their properties
- Ratios and proportion
- Decimals and percentages
- Dividing fractions by fractions
- Finding common factors and multiples
- US and metric systems of measurement

Algebra and function questions cover:

- Problem solving techniques for algebraic expressions, as well as real-life problems
- Equations and inequalities
- Solving expressions that contain one variable
- Finding equivalent expressions
- Narrative and mathematical representations of data
- Linear equations and simultaneous equations
- Graphs
- Basic functions
- Function domain and range

Geometry questions cover these skills:

- Solving problems on geometric shapes
  - Describing or drawing figures
  - Interpreting relationships between figures
  - Right triangle geometry
  - Circles
  - Real-life problems on angles, area, and volume
- Pythagorean theorem
- Using transformation and symmetry to solve problems
- Modeling problems

Statistics and probability questions cover:

- Reading and interpreting graphs, charts, and number lines
- Interpreting distributions
- Drawing conclusions based on the data provided
- Calculating mean, median, mode, and range
- Calculating basic probability
- Using random sampling to draw conclusions about data
- Understanding probability models
- Understanding the difference between statistical and non-statistical questions

Most of the questions will be multiple-choice, but there will be some numeric entry questions.

For the numeric entry questions, you have to make a calculation and provide the answer on your own. You will see a small box in which to place your answer, but you will not be provided with any answer choices.

You should also be aware that on some of the multiple-choice questions, you will be allowed to choose more than one response.

How to Use This Publication

As you work through this study guide, you will notice that Practice Test 1 is in workbook format, providing study tips and solutions after each question.

The workbook format of practice test 1 will help you learn the strategies and formulas that you need to answer all of the types of questions on the actual Praxis Core Math Test.

You can refer back to the formulas and tips introduced in the workbook as you work through the remaining material in the book.

Ideally, you should try to memorize these formulas and tips before you take the remaining practice tests in the book.

You may wish to time yourself as you do the practice tests in this book, allowing yourself 85 minutes for each exam. This will help to simulate the conditions of the actual test.

For ease of reference during your study, Practice Tests 2 and 3 are organized by skill area, so you will see all of the number and quantity questions first, followed by the algebra, geometry, and statistics and probability questions.

On the computerized version of the actual exam, the questions will not be placed into skill groups like this. Rather, the computer will deliver questions at random from any one of the four skill areas as you take the test.

The answers and solutions for Practice Tests 2 and 3 are provided at the end of each of the practice exams.

This study guide assumes knowledge of basic math skills, such as addition, subtraction, multiplication, division, percentages, and decimals.

Free Basic Math Review Problems

If you have difficulties with basic math problems or if you have been out of school for a while, you may wish to review our free basic math problems before taking the practice tests in this book.

The free review problems can be found at: www.examsam.com

4

Praxis Core Practice Math Test 1 with Workbook

Number and Quantity Problems:

1) Which of the following shows the numbers ordered from least to greatest?
   A) $-\frac{1}{4}$, $\frac{1}{8}$, $\frac{1}{6}$, 1
   B) $-\frac{1}{4}$, $\frac{1}{8}$, 1 , $\frac{1}{6}$
   C) $-\frac{1}{4}$, $\frac{1}{6}$, $\frac{1}{8}$, 1
   D) $-\frac{1}{4}$, 1 , $\frac{1}{8}$, $\frac{1}{6}$
   E) 1 , $\frac{1}{6}$, $\frac{1}{8}$, $-\frac{1}{4}$

> In order to answer questions on ordering numbers from least to greatest
> or greatest to least, remember these principles: (a) Negative numbers are
> less than positive numbers; (b) When two fractions have the same
> numerator, the fraction with the smaller number in the denominator is the
> larger fraction.

The correct answer is A.

According to the principles above, $-\frac{1}{4}$ is less than $\frac{1}{8}$, $\frac{1}{8}$ is less than $\frac{1}{6}$, and $\frac{1}{6}$ is less than 1.

2) The numbers in the following list are ordered from greatest to least:

$$\theta \, , \, \eta \, , \, {}^{25}/_{13} \, , \, {}^{10}/_9 \, , \, {}^{1}/_3$$

Which of the following could be the value of η? You may select more than one answer. Be sure to choose all possible answers.
   A) $\sqrt{36}$
   B) ${}^{25}/_{14}$
   C) ${}^{26}/_{13}$
   D) 2
   E) ${}^{1}/_4$

> This problem is asking you to determine missing values from an ordered
> list of numbers. Remember to choose all of the possible values for
> questions like this one.

The correct answers are A, C, and D.

From the facts in the problem, we know that η needs to be greater than ${}^{25}/_{13}$.

If we convert ${}^{25}/_{13}$ to decimal form, we get 1.923077.

The square root of 36 is 6, so (A) is a correct response.

5

$^{26}/_{13}$ is equal to 2, and 2 is greater than 1.923077, so (C) and (D) are also correct responses.

3) If $7x$ is between 5 and 6, which of the following could be the value of x?
   A) $^2/_3$
   B) $^3/_4$
   C) $^5/_8$
   D) $^7/_8$
   E) $^5/_9$

   > When a problem asks you to multiply a whole number by a fraction, multiply the whole number by the numerator and then divide this result by the denominator. To solve the problem, insert the fractions from the answer choices for the value of x. Then complete the multiplication and division to see which fraction meets the criteria stated in the problem.

   The correct answer is B.

   $5 < 7x < 6$

   $5 < (7 \times {}^3/_4) < 6$

   $5 < [(7 \times 3) \div 4] < 6$

   $5 < (21 \div 4) < 6$

   $5 < 5.25 < 6$

   5.25 is between 5 and 6, so $^3/_4$ is the correct answer.

4) The temperature on Saturday was 62° F at 5:00 PM and 38° F at 11:00 PM. If the temperature fell at a constant rate on Saturday, what was the temperature at 9:00 PM?
   A) 58° F
   B) 54° F
   C) 50° F
   D) 46° F
   E) 40° F

   > This question assesses your knowledge of performing operations on integers. Here, we have to perform the operations of subtraction, multiplication, and division.

   The correct answer is D.

First of all, you need to determine the difference in temperature during the entire time period: 62 – 38 = 24 degrees less

Then calculate how much time has passed. From 5:00 PM to 11:00 PM, 6 hours have passed.

Next, divide the temperature difference by the amount of time that has passed to get the temperature change per hour.

24 degrees ÷ 6 hours = 4 degrees less per hour

To calculate the temperature at the stated time, you need to calculate the time difference.

From 5:00 PM to 9:00 PM, 4 hours have passed. So, the temperature difference during the stated time is 4 hours × 4 degrees per hour = 16 degrees less.

Finally, deduct this from the beginning temperature to get your final answer.

62° F – 16° F = 46° F

5)   In the last step of doing a calculation, Adam subtracted 180 instead of adding 180. What number can Adam add to his final erroneous result in order to get the correct calculation?
A)   90
B)   180
C)   270
D)   360
E)   450

> This question assesses your knowledge of performing shortcut operations on integers in order to correct erroneous calculations.

The correct answer is D.

He subtracted 180 by mistake, so we need to add that back to correct the error. Then we need to add 180 for the original calculation that he should have done. 180 × 2 = 360

6)   A painter needs to paint 8 rooms, each of which have a surface area of 2000 square feet. If one bucket of paint covers 900 square feet, what is the fewest number of buckets of paint that must be used to complete all 8 rooms?
A)   3
B)   17
C)   18

D) 19
E) 20

This is a question that requires you to find the fewest multiples of an item. Be mindful of the words "fewest" and "greatest" in problems like this one, since it will normally be impossible to purchase a fractional part of the item in the question. Therefore, you will need to round your result up or down accordingly.

The correct answer is C.

For your first step, determine how many square feet there are in total:
2000 square feet per room × 8 rooms = 16,000 square feet in total

Then you need to divide by the coverage rate:

16,000 square feet to cover ÷ 900 square feet coverage per bucket = 17.77 buckets needed

It is not possible to purchase a partial bucket of paint, so 17.77 is rounded up to 18 buckets of paint.

7)   Soon Li jogged 3.6 miles in $^3/_4$ of an hour. What was her average jogging speed in miles per hour?
A) 2.7
B) 4.0
C) 4.2
D) 4.6
E) 4.8

This problem involves the calculation of miles per hour. To solve the problem, divide the distance traveled by the time in order to get the speed in miles per hour.

The correct answer is E.

As stated above, divide the distance traveled by the time in order to get the speed in miles per hour.

Remember that in order to divide by a fraction, you need to invert the fraction, and then multiply.

$3.6 \text{ miles} \div \, ^3/_4 =$

$3.6 \times \, ^4/_3 =$

$(3.6 \times 4) \div 3 =$

$14.4 \div 3 = 4.8$ miles per hour

8) When 1523.48 is divided by 100, which digit of the resulting number is in the tenths place?
   A) 1
   B) 2
   C) 3
   D) 4
   E) 5

> This question assesses your understanding of decimals. Remember that the number after the decimal is in the tenths place, the second number after the decimal is in the hundredths place, and the third number after the decimal is in the thousandths place.

The correct answer is B.

Perform the division, and then check the decimal places of the numbers. Divide as follows: $1523.48 \div 100 = 15.2348$

Reading our result from left to right: 1 is in the tens place, 5 is in the ones place, 2 is in the tenths place, 3 is in the hundredths place, 4 is in the thousandths place, and 8 is in the ten-thousandths place.

9) The price of a certain book is reduced from $60 to $45 at the end of the semester. By what percent is the price of the book reduced?
   A) 15%
   B) 20%
   C) 25%
   D) 33%
   E) 45%

> This question asks you to perform a calculation in order to determine the percentage discount on an item. Divide the dollar value of the reduction by the original price to get the percentage.

The correct answer is C.

Determine the dollar amount of the discount.

$60 original price – $45 sale price = $15 discount

Then divide the discount by the original price to get the percentage of the discount.

$15 ÷ $60 = 0.25 = 25%

10) Mr. Rodriguez teaches a class of 25 students. Ten of the students in his class participate in drama club. In which graph below does the dark gray area represent the percentage of students who participate in drama club?

A)

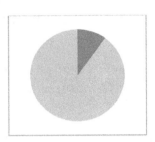

B)

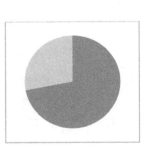

C)

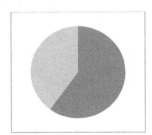

D)

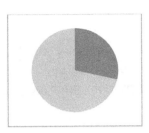

E)

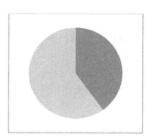

Questions like this one are asking you about how to express percentages graphically. Facts such as x students from y total students participate in a group can be represented as x/y.

The correct answer is E.

Ten out of 25 students participate in drama club.

First of all, express the relationship as a fraction: $10/25$

Then divide to find the percentage: $10/25 = 10 \div 25 = 0.40 = 40\%$

Finally, choose the pie chart that has 40% of its area shaded in dark gray.

40% is slightly less than half, so you need to choose chart E.

11) The ratio of males to females in the senior year class of Carson Heights High School was 6 to 7. If the total number of students in the class is 117, how many males are in the class?
   A) 48
   B) 54
   C) 56
   D) 58
   E) 63

Remember that a ratio can be expressed by using the word "to" or by separating the amounts in the subsets with a colon. So, our ratio is expressed as 6 to 7 or 6:7.

The correct answer is B.

For your first step, add the subsets of the ratio together: 6 + 7 = 13

Then divide this into the total: $117 \div 13 = 9$

Finally, multiply the result from the previous step by the subset of males from the ratio: $6 \times 9 = 54$ males in the class

12) Which of the following units of measure is most likely to be the height of a two story building?
A) 36 feet
B) 12 feet
C) 2 meters
D) 200 feet
E) 100 yards

> For questions asking you about units of measurement for a specific item, try to think about the scale of the item in common-sense terms. For instance, a single story of a building is usually about double the height of a person.

The correct answer is A.

We can assume that a story of a building is usually about double the height of a person.

For the sake of simplicity, we can estimate the height of a person to be 6 feet, and a height of a story of a building to be 12 feet.

So, the height of a two-story building would be 36 feet, including the height of the roof.

13) Sarah creates the following conversion: 6 yards × 3 feet/1 yard × 12 inches/1 foot
Which of the following conversions is she making?
A) Feet to yards
B) Inches to yards
C) Yards to feet
D) Yards to inches
E) Feet to inches

> For questions involving conversions of measurements, take note of the first item in the calculation, as well as the numerator of the final fraction in the conversion. In other words, for our problem:
> 6 **yards** × 3 feet/1 yard × 12 **inches**/1 foot

The correct answer is D.

Read from left to right. First of all, yards are converted to feet; then feet are converted to inches.

So, overall, yards are being converted to inches.

14) The graph below shows the relationship between the total number of hamburgers a restaurant sells and the total sales in dollars for the hamburgers. What is the sales price per hamburger?

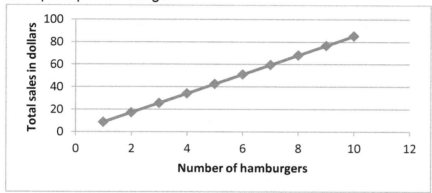

A) $4.00
B) $8.00
C) $8.50
D) $9.50
E) $10.00

This is an example of a question that asks you to interpret a graph in order to determine the price per unit of an item. To solve the problem, look at the graph and then divide the total sales in dollars by the total quantity sold in order to get the price per unit.

The correct answer is C.

For ten hamburgers, the total price is $85, so each hamburger sells for $8.50:
$85 total sales in dollars ÷ 10 hamburgers sold = $8.50 each

15) In Brown County Elementary School, parents are advised to have their children vaccinated against five childhood diseases. According to the chart below, how many children were vaccinated against at least three diseases?

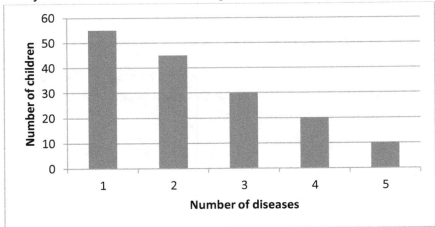

A)   30
B)   50
C)   60
D) 100
E) 130

> For number and quantity questions that ask you to interpret bar graphs, you need to read the problem carefully to determine what is represented on the horizontal axis (bottom) and the vertical axis (left side) of the graph.

The correct answer is C.

The quantity of diseases is indicated on the bottom of the graph, while the number of children is indicated on the left side of the graph.

To determine the amount of children that have been vaccinated against three or more diseases, we need to add the amounts represented by the bars for 3, 4, and 5 diseases:

30 + 20 + 10 = 60 children

16) The pictograph below shows the number of pizzas sold in one day at a local pizzeria. Cheese pizzas sold for $10 each, pepperoni pizzas sold for $12, and the total sales of all three types of pizza was $310. What is the sales price of one vegetable pizza?

Cheese	▼ ▼ ▼
Pepperoni	▼ ▼
Vegetable	▼

Each ▼ represents 5 pizzas.

A) $5
B) $8
C) $9
D) $10
E) $12

This is an example of an exam question on interpreting data from pictographs. Each symbol on the pictograph represents a certain quantity of items, so remember to multiply by that amount in order to determine the totals for each group.

The correct answer is B.

First, determine how many cheese and pepperoni pizzas were sold. Each triangle symbol represents 5 pizzas.

Therefore, 15 cheese pizzas were sold:
3 symbols on the pictograph × 5 pizzas per symbol = 15 cheese pizzas

We also know that 10 pepperoni pizzas were sold:
2 symbols on the pictograph × 5 pizzas per symbol = 10 pepperoni pizzas

Then determine the value of these two types of pizzas based on the prices stated in the problem:
(15 cheese pizzas × $10 each) + (10 pepperoni pizzas × $12 each) =
$150 + $120 = $270

The remaining amount is allocable to the vegetable pizzas:
Total sales of $310 − $270 = $40 worth of vegetable pizzas

Since each triangle represents 5 pizzas, 5 vegetable pizzas were sold. We calculate the price of the vegetable pizzas as follows:

$40 worth of vegetable pizzas ÷ 5 vegetable pizzas sold = $8 per vegetable pizza

17)   A zoo has reptiles, birds, quadrupeds, and fish. At the start of the year, they have a total of 1,500 creatures living in the zoo. The pie chart below shows percentages by category for the 1,500 creatures at the start of the year.

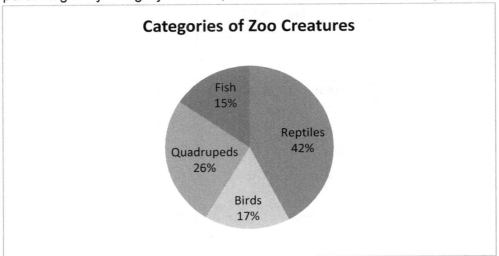

Categories of Zoo Creatures

At the end of the year, the zoo still has 1,500 creatures, but reptiles constitute 40%, birds 23%, and quadrupeds 21%. How many more fish were there at the end of the year than at the beginning of the year?

A)   10
B)   11
C)   15
D)   16
E)   150

This question is asking you to interpret a pie chart that shows percentages by category. If you are asked to calculate changes to the data in the categories in the chart, be sure to multiply by the percentages at the beginning of the year and then do a separate calculation using the percentages at the end of the year.

The correct answer is C.

At the beginning of the year, 15% of the 1,500 creatures were fish, so there were 225 fish at the beginning of the year (1,500 × 0.15 = 225).

In order to find the percentage of fish at the end of the year, we first need to add up the percentages for the other animals: 40% + 23% + 21% = 84%

Then subtract this amount from 100% to get the remaining percentage for the fish: 100% − 84% = 16%

Multiply the percentage by the total to get the number of fish at the end of the year: 1,500 × 0.16 = 240

Then subtract the beginning of the year from the end of the year to calculate the increase in the number of fish: 240 − 225 = 15

Algebra and Function Problems:

18) If $\frac{3}{4}x - 2 = 4$, $x = ?$

   A) $\frac{8}{3}$

   B) $\frac{1}{8}$

   C) 8

   D) −8

   E) 24

> This is a problem requiring you to solve an expression that contains a single variable, a fraction, and integers. First, isolate the integers and then eliminate the fraction. Finally, divide to find the value of the variable.

The correct answer is C.

Isolate the integers to one side of the equation.

$$\frac{3}{4}x - 2 = 4$$

$$\frac{3}{4}x - 2 + 2 = 4 + 2$$

$$\frac{3}{4}x = 6$$

Then get rid of the fraction by multiplying both sides by the denominator.

$$\frac{3}{4}x \times 4 = 6 \times 4$$

$$3x = 24$$

Then divide to solve the problem.

$$3x \div 3 = 24 \div 3$$

$$x = 8$$

19) If $2(3x - 1) = 4(x + 1) - 3$, what is the value of x? State your answer as a fraction in the spaces provided.

Numerator value of x = _____

Denominator value of x = _____

This problem requires you to solve an algebraic expression that contains one variable (x) on both sides of the equation. When the variable is used on both sides of the equation, you should perform the multiplication on the parentheticals first. Then isolate x to solve the problem.

The correct answers are 3 (numerator value) and 2 (denominator value).

Perform the multiplication on the terms in the parentheses.
$2(3x - 1) = 4(x + 1) - 3$
$6x - 2 = (4x + 4) - 3$

Then simplify.
$6x - 2 = (4x + 4) - 3$
$6x - 2 = 4x + 1$
$6x - 2 - 1 = 4x + 1 - 1$
$6x - 3 = 4x$

Then isolate x to get your answer.
$6x - 3 = 4x$
$6x - 4x - 3 = 4x - 4x$
$2x - 3 = 0$
$2x - 3 + 3 = 0 + 3$
$2x = 3$
$2x \div 2 = 3 \div 2$
$x = {}^3/_2$

20)   If $x + y = 5$ and $a + b = 4$, what is the value of $(3x + 3y)(5a + 5b)$?
A)   9
B)   35
C) 200
D) 300
E) 350

This problem involves expressions that contain more than one variable. First of all, factor each parenthetical in the final expression. Then substitute values in order to solve the problem.

The correct answer is D.

Factor each of the parentheticals in the expression provided in the problem:

$(3x + 3y)(5a + 5b) =$

$3(x + y) \times 5(a + b)$

We know that $x + y = 5$ and $a + b = 4$, so we can substitute the values stated for each of the parentheticals:

$3(x + y) \times 5(a + b) =$

$3(5) \times 5(4) =$

$15 \times 20 = 300$

21) Consider the inequality: $-3x + 14 < 5$
Which of the following values of x are possible solutions to the inequality above? You may select more than one answer.
A) −3.1
B) 2.80
C) 2.25
D) 3.15
E) 4.35

> This question is assessing your understanding of inequalities. When dealing with inequalities, we first need to place the integers on one side of the inequality. Then deal with any negative numbers. Remember that when you divide or multiply by a negative number in inequality problems, you need to reverse the way that the inequality sign points.

The correct answers are D and E.

Place the integers on one side of the inequality.
$-3x + 14 < 5$
$-3x + 14 - 14 < 5 - 14$
$-3x < -9$

Then get rid of the negative number. We need to reverse the way that the inequality sign points because we are dividing.
$-3x < -9$
$-3x \div -3 > -9 \div -3$ ("Less than" becomes "greater than" because we divide by a negative number.)
$x > 3$

3.15 and 4.35 are greater than 3, so they are the correct answers.

22) Which of the following equations is equivalent to $\frac{x}{5} + \frac{y}{2}$?
A) $\frac{x + y}{7}$

B) $\frac{2x + 5y}{10}$

C) $\dfrac{5x+2y}{10}$

D) $\dfrac{2x+5y}{7}$

E) $\dfrac{5y}{2x}$

> This problem is asking you to find an equivalent expression for a
> mathematical equation that contains fractions. To add fractions, find the
> lowest common denominator first and then add the numerators.

The correct answer is B.

You need to find the lowest common denominator. Then add the numerators
together as shown.

$$\dfrac{x}{5} + \dfrac{y}{2} =$$

$$\left(\dfrac{x}{5} \times \dfrac{2}{2}\right) + \left(\dfrac{y}{2} \times \dfrac{5}{5}\right) =$$

$$\dfrac{2x}{10} + \dfrac{5y}{10} =$$

$$\dfrac{2x + 5y}{10}$$

23) Which of the following steps will solve the equation for x: $4x - 3 = 2$
A) Add 3 to both sides of the equation, and then divide both sides by 4.
B) Add 3 to both sides of the equation, and then subtract 4 from both sides.
C) Add 2 to both sides of the equation, and then divide both sides by 4.
D) Subtract 2 from both sides of the equation, and then divide both sides by −3.
E) Divide both sides of the equations by 4, and then subtract 3 from both sides.

> For this question, you need to find the answer that provides a narrative
> explanation for the solution to the problem, rather than calculating the
> solution itself.

The correct answer is A.

Remember that to solve problems like this, you need to deal with the integers
(whole numbers) and then isolate the variable (x).

The solution is as follows:

$4x - 3 = 2$

$4x - 3 + 3 = 2 + 3$ (Add 3 to both sides of the equation.)

$4x = 5$

$4x \div 4 = 5 \div 4$ (Divide both sides by 4.)

$x = \frac{5}{4}$

24) Shanika works as a car salesperson. She earns $1,000 a month, plus $390 for each car she sells. If she wants to earn at least $4,000 this month, what is the minimum number of cars that she must sell this month? Please write your answer in the space provided.

_____ cars to sell this month

> This question requires using problem solving techniques to solve real-life problems. For problems like this one, read the facts carefully and set up an equation to find the missing variable or quantity.

The correct answer is 8 cars.

Shanika wants to earn $4,000 this month.

She gets the $1,000 basic pay regardless of the number of cars she sells, so we need to subtract that from the total first:

$4,000 – $1,000 = $3,000

She gets $390 for each car she sells, so we need to divide that into the remaining $3,000:

$3,000 to earn ÷ $390 per car = 7.69 cars to sell

Since it is not possible to sell a part of a car, we need to round up to 8 cars.

Alternatively, we could have solved the problem by using the following algebraic expression:

$4,000 = $1,000 + ($390 × x)

$3,000 ÷ $390 = x

25) Toby is going to buy a car. The total purchase price of the car is represented by variable C. He will pay D dollars immediately, and then he will make equal payments (P) each month for a certain number of months (M). Which equation below represents the amount of his monthly payment (P)?

A) $\frac{C-D}{M}$

B) $\frac{C}{M} - D$

C) $\frac{M}{C-D}$

D) $D - \frac{C}{M}$

E) $\frac{C}{M}$

This problem requires you to set up an algebraic equation based on facts in a real-life problem. In this problem, we need to calculate a monthly payment after a down payment has been made. Deduct the down payment from the purchase price, and then divide by the number of months to solve the problem.

The correct answer is A.

The total amount that Toby has to pay is represented by C.

He is paying D dollars immediately, so we can determine the remaining amount that he owes by deducting his down payment from the total.

So, the remaining amount owing is represented by the equation: C – D

We have to divide the remaining amount owing by the number of months (M) to get the monthly payment (P):

P = (C – D) ÷ M = $\frac{C-D}{M}$

26) Fatima drove into town at a rate of 50 miles per hour. She shopped in town for 20 minutes, and then drove home on the same route at a rate of 60 miles per hour. Which of the following equations best expresses the total time (Tt) that it took Fatima to make the journey and do the shopping? Note that the variable D represents the distance in miles from Fatima's house to town.

A) $Tt + 20 \text{ minutes} = 110 \times D$

B) $Tt + 20 \text{ minutes} = [(50 + 60) \div 2] \times D$

C) $Tt = [(D \div 50) + (D \div 60)] + 20 \text{ minutes}$

D) $Tt = D \div 110$

E) $Tt = (D \div 110) + 20 \text{ minutes}$

> This problem asks you to set up an algebraic equation based on facts in a real-life problem. In this problem, we need to calculate the time spent on a journey. Read the problem carefully and make sure that all of the required facts are represented in your final equation.

The correct answer is C.

The amount of time in hours (T) multiplied by miles per hour (mph) gives us the distance traveled (D).

So, the equation for distance traveled is: $T \times \text{mph} = D$

The problem tells us that we need to calculate T, so we need to isolate T by changing our equation as follows:

$T \times \text{mph} = D$

$(T \times \text{mph}) \div \text{mph} = D \div \text{mph}$

$T = D \div \text{mph}$

In our problem, Fatima drives home on the same route that she took into town, so we need to calculate the traveling time for the journey into town, as well as for the journey home:

$(D \div 50) + (D \div 60) = T$

Then add back the 20 minutes she spent in town to get the total time:

$Tt = [(D \div 50) + (D \div 60)] + 20 \text{ minutes}$

27) A baseball team sells T-shirts and sweatpants to the public for a fundraising event. The total amount of money the team earned from these sales was $850. Variable *t* represents the number of T-shirts sold and variable *s* represents the number of sweatpants sold. The total sales in dollars is represented by the equation $25t + 30s$. The amount earned by selling sweatpants is what fraction of the total amount earned?

A) *s*/850

B) 30*s*/850

C) (25*t* + 30*s*)/850

D) *t*/850

E) 25*t*/850

This problem asks you to express part of an algebraic equation as a fraction of the entire equation. You can sometimes substitute a numerical or dollar value for the entire expression, as in this problem.

The correct answer is B.

We need to set up a fraction, the numerator of which consists of the amount of sales in dollars for sweatpants, and the denominator of which consists of the total amount of sales in dollars for both items.

The problem tells us that the amount of sales in dollars for sweatpants is 30*s* and the total amount of sales is 850, so the answer is 30*s*/850.

28) 2 inches on a scale drawing represents *F* feet. Which of the following equations represents *F* + 1 feet on the drawing?

A) $\dfrac{2(F+1)}{F}$

B) $\dfrac{(F+1)}{F}$

C) $\dfrac{2}{F+1}$

D) $\dfrac{2F}{F+1}$

E) $\dfrac{(F+1)}{2}$

This question requires you to set up simultaneous equations for a scale drawing. Set up ratios for each of the measurements, and then cross multiply to solve.

The correct answer is A.

We know that 2 inches represents F feet. We can set this up as a ratio $2/F$.

Next, we need to calculate the ratio for $F + 1$. The number of inches that represents $F + 1$ is unknown, so we will refer to this unknown as x.

So we have:

$$\frac{2}{F} = \frac{x}{F + 1}$$

Now cross multiply.

$$\frac{2}{F} = \frac{x}{F + 1}$$

$$F \times x = 2 \times (F + 1)$$

$$Fx = 2(F + 1)$$

Then isolate x to solve.

$$Fx \div F = [2(F + 1)] \div F$$

$$x = \frac{2(F + 1)}{F}$$

29) The speed of sound in a recent experiment was 340,000 millimeters per second. How far did the sound travel in 1,000 seconds?
   A) 3.4×10^4 millimeters
   B) 3.4×10^5 millimeters
   C) 3.4×10^5 millimeters
   D) 3.4×10^7 millimeters
   E) 3.4×10^8 millimeters

> This problem involves identifying an equivalent expression in scientific notation. Scientific notation means that you give the expression as the result of two products: one of which contains a decimal and the other of which contains 10 to an exponential power. The exponent of the 10 is the number of places that the decimal point must be shifted in order to give the number in long form.

The correct answer is E.

Be careful with your zeroes. We are taking 340,000 (4 zeroes) times 1,000 (three zeroes).

The result is: 340,000 × 1,000 = 340,000,000 = 34 × 10,000,000 (seven zeroes)

However, our answer choices are expressed with 3.4, not 34.

So, we will need to have to multiply by a figure with 8 zeroes to account for the change in the position of the decimal.

3.4×10^8 millimeters = 3.4 × 100,000,000 millimeters = 340,000,000

30) A mother has noticed that the more sugar her child eats, the more her child sleeps at night. Which of the following graphs best illustrates the relationship between the amount of sugar the child consumes and the child's amount of sleep?

A)

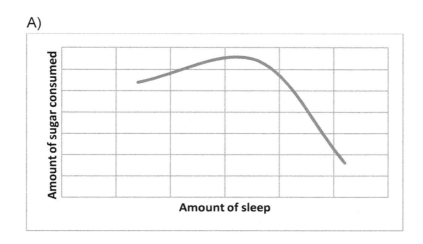

B)

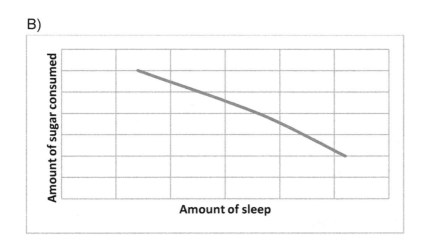

C)

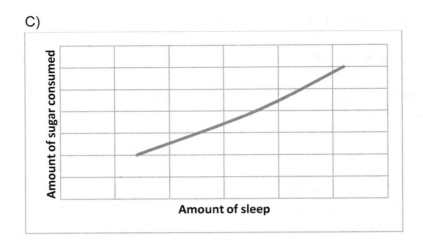

D)

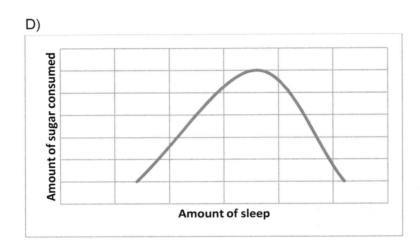

E)

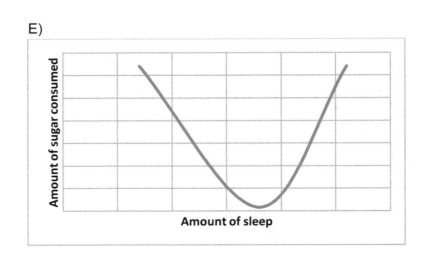

Your exam will have problems like this one that show line graphs of linear equations. Be sure that you know the difference between positive linear relationships and negative linear relationships for the exam. In a positive linear relationship, an increase in one variable causes an increase in the other variable, meaning that the line will point upwards from left to right.

In a negative linear relationship, an increase in one variable causes a decrease in the other variable, meaning that the line will point downwards from left to right.

The correct answer is C.

As the quantity of sugar increases, the amount of sleep also increases.

A positive linear relationship therefore exists between the two variables. This is represented in chart C since the amount of sleep is greater when the amount of sugar consumed is higher.

31)   Which one of the scatterplots below most strongly suggests a negative linear relationship between x and y?

A)

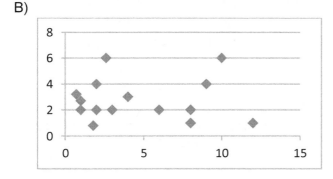

B)

C)

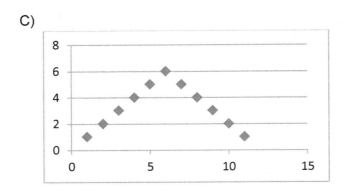

D)

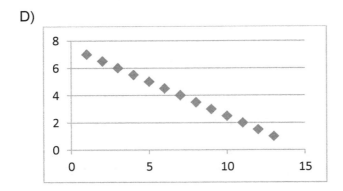

E)

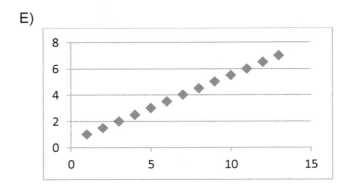

Your exam will have problems containing scatterplots like those above. For these types of questions, you will need to look at each scatterplot and determine which one has the dots in a configuration most similar to the one in the question. As stated in the previous problem, be sure that you know the difference between positive linear relationships and negative linear relationships for the exam.

The correct answer is D.

A negative linear relationship exists when an increase in one variable results in a decrease in the other variable. This is represented by chart D.

32) The graph of a linear equation is shown below. Which one of the tables of values best represents the points on the graph?

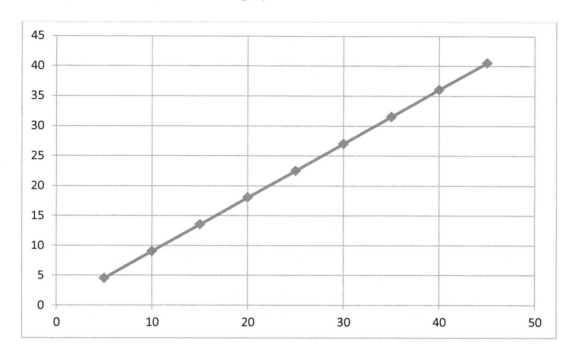

A)

x	y
5	5
10	10
15	15
20	20

B)

x	y
5	4
10	8
15	12
20	16

C)

x	y
5	4.5
10	9
15	13.5
20	18

D)

x	y
5	9
10	13
15	15
20	20

E)

x	y
0	0
5	4.5
10	9
15	13.5

This is an example of an exam question involving basic functions. A function expresses the mathematical relationship between x and y. So, a certain recurring mathematical operation on x will yield a result of y. To solve problems like this one, look carefully at the point that is furthest to the left on the graph. You will be able to eliminate several of the answer choices because they will not state this first coordinate correctly. Then try to work out the relationship between the coordinates of the first point to those of the next point on the line. Use the horizontal and vertical grid lines on the graph to help you.

The correct answer is C.

We can see that the line does not begin on exactly on (5, 5), nor does it begin on (5, 9) or (0,0) because the first point is slightly below the horizontal line for $y = 5$.

Therefore, we can rule out answers A, D, and E.

If we look at $x = 20$ on the graph, we can see that $y = 18$ at this point.

We can express this as the function: $\int(x) = x \times 0.9$

Putting in the values of x from chart (C), we get the following:

$5 \times 0.9 = 4.5$

$10 \times 0.9 = 9$

$15 \times 0.9 = 13.5$

20 × 0.9 = 18

So, C is the correct answer.

33) An airplane flew at a constant speed, traveling 780 miles in 2 hours. The graph below shows the total miles the airplane traveled in 20 minute intervals. According to the graph, how many miles did the plane travel in the last 40 minutes of its journey?

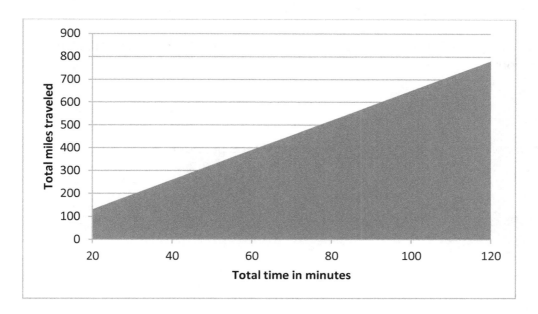

A) 120
B) 180
C) 200
D) 260
E) 380

This problem asks you to interpret a graph of the domain (x) and range (y) of a function. These types of problems will have two variables. In the graph above, variable x is the total time and variable y is the total miles traveled.

The correct answer is D.

The last 40 minutes of the journey begin at the 80 minute mark and end at the 120 minute mark.

The line for 80 minutes is at 520 miles and the line for 120 minutes is at 780 miles, so the plane has traveled 260 miles (780 − 520 = 260) in the last 40 minutes.

Alternatively, we can use the function that this graph represents to solve the problem.

First, we can perform division to determine that the plane travels 6.5 miles per minute.

For example, the line for 120 minutes is at 780 miles:

$$780 \text{ miles} \div 120 \text{ minutes} = 6.5 \text{ miles per minute}$$

Since the plane is travelling at a constant rate, the graph above expresses the function:

$$\int (x) = x \times 6.5$$

So, for we can put 40 minutes in for x to solve the problem.

$$\int (x) = x \times 6.5 = 40 \times 6.5 = 260$$

34)

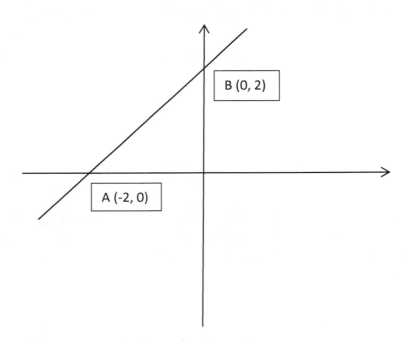

The line in the xy plane above is going to be shifted 5 units to the left and 4 units up. What are the coordinates of point B after the shift?

A) (−5, 6)
B) (5, 6)
C) (5, 4)
D) (−7, 4)
E) (7, 6)

This question involves transposing the coordinates of a linear equation.

Remember these rules on transpositions:

x coordinate moved to the left – deduct the units from the original x coordinate

x coordinate moved to the right – add the units to the original x coordinate

y coordinate moved down – deduct the units from the original y coordinate

y coordinate moved up – add the units to the original y coordinate

---

The correct answer is A.

We start off with point B, which is represented by the coordinates (0, 2).

The line is then shifted 5 units to the left and 4 units up. When we go to the left, we need to deduct the units, and when we go up we need to add units.

So, do the operations on each of the coordinates in order to solve: $0 - 5 = -5$ and $2 + 4 = 6$, so our new coordinates are (−5, 6).

Geometry Problems:

35) The line on the *xy*-graph below forms the diameter of the circle. What is the area of the circle?

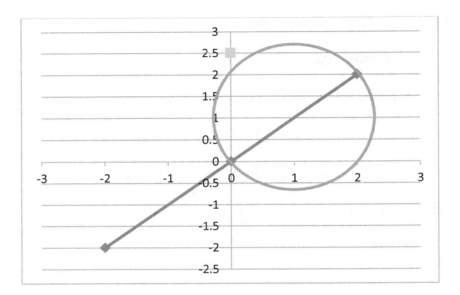

A) π

B) 2π

C) $\frac{\pi}{2}$

D) 2.5π

E) 1.5625π

To solve this problem, you will need the formulas for hypotenuse length, radius, and area.

Hypotenuse length: $\sqrt{A^2 + B^2} = C$

Radius of a circle = ½ × diameter

Area of a circle = $\pi R^2 = \pi \times$ radius^2

See page 41 for a further explanation of the Pythagorean Theorem.

The correct answer is B.

The line that represents the diameter of the circle forms the hypotenuse of a triangle. Side A of the triangle begins on (0, 0) and ends on (0, 2), with a length of 2. Side B of the triangle begins on (0, 2) and ends on (2, 2), so it also has a length of 2. So, the diameter of the circle is: $\sqrt{2^2 + 2^2} = \sqrt{8} = \sqrt{4 \times 2} = 2\sqrt{2}$

Next, we need to calculate the radius of the circle. The radius of the circle is $\sqrt{2}$ because the diameter is $2\sqrt{2}$ and the formula for the radius of a circle is ½ × diameter = radius.

Finally, we can use the formula for the area of a circle to solve the problem:

$\pi\sqrt{2}^2 = 2\pi$

36) A small circle has a radius of 5 inches, and a larger circle has a radius of 8 inches. What is the difference in inches between the circumferences of the two circles?
A) 3
B) 6
C) 6π
D) 9π
E) 39π

The question above is asking you to calculate the circumference of two circles. The formula for the circumference of a circle is:

Circumference of a circle = $2\pi R$ = (2 × π × radius)

The correct answer is C.

Use the formula from above: (2 × π × radius)

So, we calculate the circumference of the large circle as: 2 × π × 8 = 16π

The circumference of the small circle is: 2 × π × 5 = 10π

Then, we subtract to get our solution: 16π – 10π = 6π

37) An arc subtends an angle of 45 degrees. The angle lies at the center of a circle. The arc measures 6π. What calculations can be made on the basis of the data provided? You may select more than one response.

_____ (1) The length of the radius of the circle

_____ (2) The length of the diameter of the circle

_____ (3) The circumference of the circle

_____ (4) The area of the circle

This question is asking you about arcs. You can think of an arc as a segment of a circle. The circle below illustrates an arc that subtends an angle of 45°.

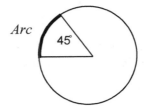

The correct answers are: 1, 2, 3, and 4.

The subtended angle measures 45 degrees.

Since there are 360 degrees in a circle, we know that 8 such arcs lie on this circle: 360 ÷ 45 = 8

So, we can calculate the circumference of the circle by multiplying the measurement of the arc, which is 6π, by 8: $6\pi \times 8 = 48\pi$ circumference

Since the formula for the circumference of a circle is $2\pi R$, we can work backwards to find the radius:

$2\pi R = 48\pi$

$2\pi R \div 2\pi = 48\pi \div 2\pi$

$R = 24$

Since we have the radius, we can also calculate the diameter:

24 × 2 = 48 diameter

We can also calculate the area:

$\pi \times \text{radius}^2 = \pi 24^2 = 576\pi$

38) Which of the following statements about isosceles triangles is true?
   A) Isosceles triangles have two equal sides.
   B) When an altitude is drawn in an isosceles triangle, two equilateral triangles are formed.
   C) The base of an isosceles triangle must be shorter than the length of each of the other two sides.
   D) The sum of the measurements of the interior angles of an isosceles triangle must be equal to 360°.
   E) If two sides of an isosceles triangle are equal, the angles opposite them are right triangles.

This question assesses your knowledge of the rules for triangles and angles.

Remember these principles on angles and triangles for your exam:

The sum of all three angles in any triangle must be equal to 180 degrees.

An isosceles triangle has two equal sides and two equal angles.

An equilateral triangle has three equal sides and three equal angles.

Angles that have the same measurement in degrees are called congruent angles.

Equilateral triangles are sometimes called congruent triangles.

Two angles are supplementary if they add up to 180 degrees. This means that when the two angles are placed together, they will form a straight line on one side.

Two angles are complementary (sometimes called adjacent angles) if they add up to 90 degrees. This means that the two angles will form a right triangle.

When two parallel lines are cut by a transversal (a straight line that runs through both of the parallel lines), 4 pairs of opposite (non-adjacent) angles are formed and 4 pairs of corresponding angles are formed. The opposite angles will be equal in measure, and the corresponding angles will also be equal in measure.

A parallelogram is a four-sided figure in which opposite sides are parallel and equal in length. Each angle will have the same measurement as the angle opposite to it, so a parallelogram has two pairs of opposite angles.

The sides of a 30° - 60° - 90° triangle are in the ratio of $1 : \sqrt{3} : 2$.

The correct answer is A. As stated above, an isosceles triangle has two equal sides, so answer A is correct.

If an altitude is drawn in an isosceles triangle, we have to put a straight line down the middle of the triangle from the peak to the base. Dividing the triangle in this way would form two right triangles, rather than two equilateral triangles. So, answer B is incorrect.

The base of an isosceles triangle can be longer than the length of each of the other two sides, so answer C is incorrect.

The sum of all three angles of any triangle must be 180 degrees, rather than 360 degrees. So, answer D is incorrect.

By definition a triangle must have three sides. Also remember that all three angles inside the triangle must add up to 180 degrees and that right angles measure 90 degrees.

Therefore, the angles opposite the two equal sides of an isosceles triangle cannot be right triangles because $2 \times 90° = 180°$. In this case, there would be no room for the third angle. So, answer E is incorrect.

39) The diagram below depicts a cell phone tower. The height of the tower from point B at the center of its base to point T at the top is 30 meters, and the distance from point B of the tower to point A on the ground is 18 meters. What is the approximate distance from point A on the ground to the top (T) of the cell phone tower?

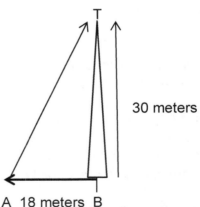

30 meters

A 18 meters B

A) 10 meters
B) 20 meters
C) 30 meters
D) 35 meters
E) 40 meters

We need to use the Pythagorean theorem to solve the problem. The Pythagorean theorem deals with right triangles. The theorem helps us to calculate the length of the hypotenuse, which is the side opposite the right angle (The right angle is at the $90°$ corner of the triangle.) The hypotenuse is called side C in the formula for the Pythagorean theorem. The theorem states that the length of the hypotenuse is equal to the square root of the sum of the squares of the lengths of the two other sides (A and B). So, we use the following formula to calculate the length of the hypotenuse:

$$\sqrt{A^2 + B^2} = C$$

The correct answer is D.

In our problem we know that one side of the triangle is 18 meters and the other side of the triangle is 30 meters, so we can put these values into the formula in order to solve the problem.

$\sqrt{A^2 + B^2} = C$

$\sqrt{18^2 + 30^2} = C$

$\sqrt{324 + 900} = C$

$\sqrt{1224} = C$

35 × 35 = 1225

So, the square root of 1224 is approximately 35.

$35 \approx C$

40) The figure below shows a right triangular prism. Side AB measures 3.5 units, side AC measures 4 units, and side BD measures 5 units. What amount below best approximates the total surface area of this triangular prism in square units?

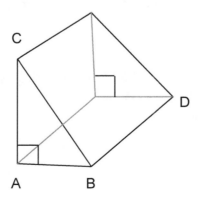

A) 66.5

B) 72.85

C) 74

D) 78.00

E) 86.85

This question is evaluating your knowledge of how to calculate the area of a right triangular prism, which is composed of both rectangles and triangles. You will again need the Pythagorean theorem for this problem, as well as the formulas for the area of rectangles and the area of triangles.

Area of a rectangle = L × W = Length × Width

Area of a triangle = $bH \div 2$ = base × height ÷ 2

The correct answer is D.

The prism has 5 sides, so we need to calculate the surface area of each one.

The rectangle at the bottom of the prism that lies along points, A, B, and D measures 3.5 units (side AB) by 5 units (side BD), so the surface area of the bottom rectangle is:

Length × Width = $3.5 \times 5 = 17.5$

Then calculate the area of the rectangle at the back of the triangle, lying along points A and C. This rectangle measures 4 units (side AC) by 5 units (the side that is parallel to side BD). So, the area of this side is:

Length × Width = $4 \times 5 = 20$

Next we need to find the length of the hypotenuse (side CB). Since AB is 3.5 units and AC is 4 units, we can use the Pythagorean theorem as follows:

$$\sqrt{3.5^2 + 4^2} = \sqrt{12.25 + 16} = \sqrt{28.25} \approx 5.3$$

We can then calculate the surface area of the sloping rectangle that lies along the hypotenuse (along points C, B and D) as:

Length × Width = $5.3 \times 5 = 26.5$

Next, we need to calculate the surface area of the two triangles on each end of the prism. The formula for the area of a triangle is $bH \div 2$, so substituting the values we get:

$(3.5 \times 4) \div 2 = 7$

Finally, add the area of all five sides together to get the surface area for the entire prism: $17.5 + 20 + 26.5 + 7 + 7 = 78$

41) Which of the following dimensions would be needed in order to find the area of the figure?

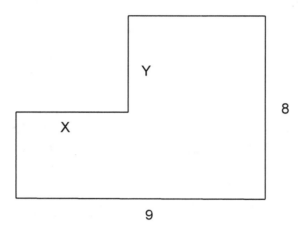

A) X only
B) Y only
C) Both X and Y
D) Either X or Y
E) Neither X nor Y

This question is asking you to calculate the area of a hybrid shape. To solve problems like this one, try to visualize two rectangles. The first rectangle would measure 8 × 9 and the second rectangle would measure X × Y.

Although not needed for this problem, you will also need to know how to find the area of a trapezoid for the exam. To calculate the area of a trapezoid, we take the average of the length of the top (T) and bottom (B) and multiply by the height (H):

$$\text{Area of a trapezoid} = \frac{T+B}{2} \times H$$

The correct answer is C.

Essentially a rectangle is missing at the upper left-hand corner of the figure.

We would need to know both the length and width of the "missing" rectangle in order to calculate the area of our figure.

So, we need to know both X and Y in order to solve the problem.

42)   The area of a square is 64 square units. This square is made up of smaller squares that measure 4 square units each. How many of the smaller squares are needed to make up the larger square?

A)   8
B)   12
C)   16
D)   24
E)   32

> This question is asking you to determine the relationships between square figures of different sizes. For problems about placing small squares inside a larger square, you can simply divide the size of the smaller squares into the size of the larger square in order to determine how many small squares are required.

The correct answer is C.

We simply divide to get the answer: 64 ÷ 4 = 16

43)   The base (B) of the cylinder in the illustration shown below is at a right angle to its sides. The radius (R) of the base of cylinder measures 5 centimeters. A circular plane that is perpendicular to the base is placed inside the cylinder. Which of the following could be true about this perpendicular circular plane?

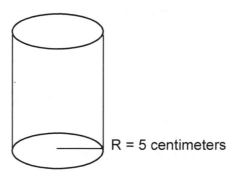

R = 5 centimeters

A) Its radius is equal to R.
B) Its radius is greater than 5.
C) Its radius is greater than 10.
D) It will be double the size of B.
E) It will be in the shape of an ellipse.

This question is asking you to interpret relationships between cylindrical and circular figures. In this question, the relationship involves right angle geometry. Remember that if two planes are perpendicular, a right angle is formed where the two planes meet. If two planes form a right angle within a cylinder, then the radius of the base of the cylinder will need to be equal to or greater than the radius of the figure that is to be inserted into the cylinder.

Although not needed for this problem, you should also learn the formula to calculate the volume of a cylinder:

$$\text{Volume of cylinder} = \pi R^2 h = \pi \times radius^2 \times height$$

The correct answer is A.

The circular plane is perpendicular to the base of the cylinder, so a right angle is formed.

Therefore, the perpendicular circular plane would need to be equal or lesser in size to the bottom of the cylinder in order for it to fit inside the cylinder.

So, the radius of the perpendicular circular plane would need to be equal to or less than the radius of the base of the cylinder. Therefore, the radius of the perpendicular cylinder could be equal to R.

44) The illustration below shows a right circular cone. The entire cone has a base radius of 9 and a height of 18.

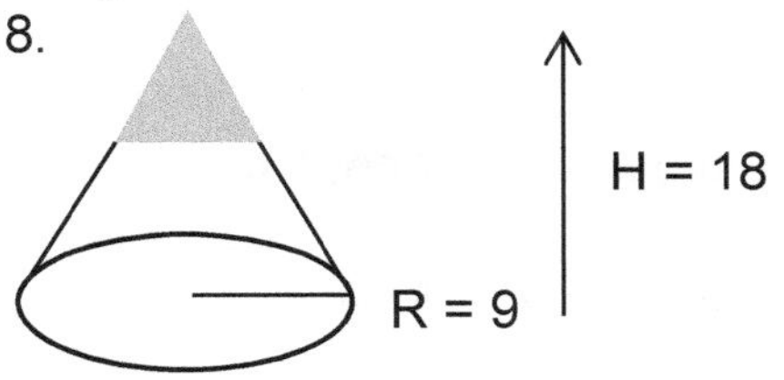

H = 18

R = 9

The shaded portion at the top of the cone has a height of 6. What fraction expresses the volume of the shaded portion to the volume of the entire cone?

State your answer as a fraction in the spaces provided.

Numerator value = _____

Denominator value = _____

This question is asking you to calculate the volume of a cone.

The formula for the volume of a cone is:

$$\frac{\pi R^2 H}{3}$$

(π × radius squared × height) ÷ 3

The correct answers are a numerator of 18 and a denominator of 486.

Another possible answer is a numerator of 1 and a denominator of 27.

First, we need to calculate the volume of the entire cone:

$(\pi \times 9^2 \times 18) \div 3 = 486\pi$

Then, we need to calculate the radius of the shaded portion. Since the height of the shaded portion is 6 and the height of the entire cone is 18, we know by using the rules of similarity that the ratio of the radius of the shaded portion to the radius of the entire cone is $^6/_{18}$ or $^1/_3$. Using this fraction, we can calculate the radius for the shaded portion. The radius of the entire cone is 9, so the radius of the shaded portion is 3:

$9 \times ^1/_3 = 3$

Then, calculate the volume of the shaded portion:

$(\pi \times 3^2 \times 6) \div 3 = 18\pi$

So, we can express the volume of the shaded portion to the volume of the entire cone as: $^{18}/_{486}$

Alternatively, we can simplify this to $^1/_{27}$.

45) The illustration below shows a right trapezoidal prism with a base width (B) of 7, a base length (L) of 8, a top width (A) of 5 and a height from base to top (H) of 3. What is the volume of the prism?

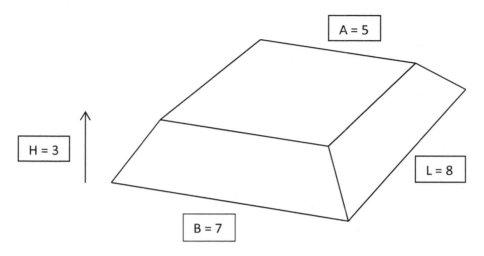

A) 56
B) 84
C) 120
D) 144
E) 168

The volume of a right trapezoidal prism is calculated by taking the average of the top and bottom widths times the base length times the height. So, we use this formula to calculate the volume:

Volume of a trapezoidal prism = [(A + B) ÷ 2] × H × L =

Average of the top width and base width × Height from base to top × Base length

Although not needed for this problem, you will also need to know how to calculate the volume of a pyramid for your exam. The volume of a pyramid is calculated by taking one-third of the base area times the height:

Volume of a pyramid: $Base\ area \times H \times \frac{1}{3}$

The correct answer is D.

Substitute the values from the illustration in order to solve the problem.

[(A + B) ÷ 2] × H × L = volume

[(5 + 7) ÷ 2] × 3 × 8 = volume

6 × 3 × 8 = 144

Statistics and Probability Problems:

46) The ages of 5 siblings are: 2, 5, 7, 12, and x. If the mean age of the 5 siblings is 8 years old, what is the age (x) of the 5th sibling?
A) 8
B) 10
C) 12
D) 14
E) 16

> This is a problem on determining the value that is missing from the calculation of a mean of a set of values. Remember that the mean is the same thing as the arithmetic average. In order to calculate the mean, you simply add up the values of all of the items in the set, and then divide by the number of items in the set. To solve problems like this one, set up an equation to calculate the mean, using x for the unknown value.

The correct answer is D.

Set up your equation to calculate the average, using x for the age of the 5th sibling:

$(2 + 5 + 7 + 12 + x) \div 5 = 8$

$(2 + 5 + 7 + 12 + x) \div 5 \times 5 = 8 \times 5$

$(2 + 5 + 7 + 12 + x) = 40$

$26 + x = 40$

$26 - 26 + x = 40 - 26$

$x = 14$

47) Members of a weight loss group report their individual weight loss to the group leader every week. During the week, the following amounts in pounds were reported: 1, 1, 3, 2, 4, 3, 1, 2, and 1. What is the mode of the weight loss for the group?
A) 1 pound
B) 2 pounds
C) 3 pounds
D) 4 pounds
E) 18 pounds

This is a question on mode. Mode is the value that occurs most frequently in a data set. For example, if 10 students scored 85 on a test, 6 students scored 90, and 4 students scored 80, the mode score is 85.

The correct answer is A.

The mode is the number that occurs the most frequently in the set.

Our data set is: 1, 1, 3, 2, 4, 3, 1, 2, 1.

The number 1 occurs 4 times in the set, which is more frequently than any other number in the set, so the mode is 1.

48) Mark's record of times for the 400 meter freestyle at swim meets this season is:

8.19, 7.59, 8.25, 7.35, 9.10

What is the median of his times?
A) 7.59
B) 8.19
C) 8.25
D) 8.096
E) 40.48

This question is asking you to find the median of a set of numbers. The median is the number that is in the middle of the set when the numbers are in ascending order.

The correct answer is B.

The problem provides the number set: 8.19, 7.59, 8.25, 7.35, 9.10

First of all, put the numbers in ascending order: 7.35, 7.59, 8.19, 8.25, 9.10

Then find the one that is in the middle: 7.35, 7.59, **8.19**, 8.25, 9.10

49) A student receives the following scores on her assignments during the term:

98.5, 85.5, 80.0, 97, 93, 92.5, 93, 87, 88, 82

What is the range of her scores?
A) 17.0
B) 18.0
C) 18.5

D) 89.65

E) 93.0

> This is a question on calculating range. To calculate range, the lowest value in the data set is deducted from the highest value in the data set.

The correct answer is C.

To calculate the range, the low number in the set is deducted from the high number in the set.

The problem set is: 98.5, 85.5, 80.0, 97, 93, 92.5, 93, 87, 88, 82.

The high number is 98.5 and the low number is 80, so the range is 18.5

$98.5 - 80 = 18.5$

50) The median and mean of 9 numbers are 8 and 9 respectively. The 9 numbers are positive integers greater than zero. If each of the 9 numbers is increased by 2, which of the following must be true of the increased numbers?

A) The mean will be greater than before, but the median will remain the same.

B) The median will be greater than before, but the mean will remain the same.

C) Both the median and mean will be greater than before.

D) The median and mean will be the same as before, but the range will increase.

E) The median, mean, and range will increase.

> This is a question on interpreting distributions. Distribution is a measurement of how spread out the data is. Remember that for these types of questions, the quantity of items in the data set will usually not change. The question will normally state that all of the values in the set are going to increase or decrease by a certain amount. If all of the values in a data set are positive integers greater than zero and all of the values increase, the mean and median will also increase, but the range will not change. Conversely, if all of the values in such a data set decrease, the mean and median will also decrease, but the range will not change.

The correct answer is C.

If each number in the set is increased by 2, the mean will increase by 2 since the overall increase in the total of the values ($2 \times 9 = 18$) will be divided equally among all nine items in the set ($18 \div 9 = 2$) when the mean is calculated.

Since each of the numbers increases by 2, the median number will also increase by 2.

51) Which of the following number lines represents seven values in which the median of the values exceeds the mean of the values?

A)

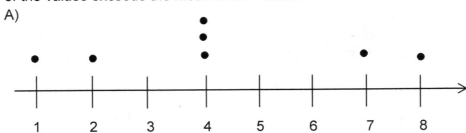

B)

C)

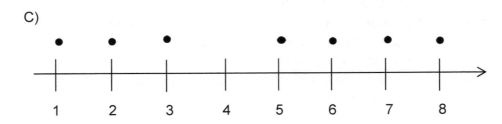

D)

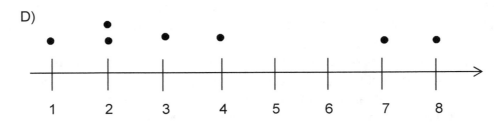

E)

52

This is a question on reading number lines to interpret distributions. To determine the distribution, you should first look to see how many dots there are above the lines. Then add up the individual values from each line to calculate the mean of each of the five answer options. You can determine the median visually by seeing which number is midway on each of the lines.

The correct answer is C.

The mean is the average of all of the numbers in the set. If we look at each of the answers, we can see that we have seven values in each set because there are seven dots above each of the number lines.

The mean for answer choice C is 4.57 and the median is 5.

Mean: $1 + 2 + 3 + 5 + 6 + 7 + 8 = 32$; $32 \div 7 = 4.57$

Median: 1, 2, 3, **5**, 6, 7, 8

So, the median exceeds the mean for the set represented on number line (C).

52) An owner of a carnival attraction draws teddy bears out of a bag at random to give to prize winners. She has 10 brown teddy bears, 8 white teddy bears, 4 black teddy bears, and 2 pink teddy bears when she opens the attraction at the start of the day. The first prize winner of the day receives a brown teddy bear. What is the probability that the second prize winner will receive a pink teddy bear?

A) $^1/_{24}$

B) $^1/_{23}$

C) $^2/_{24}$

D) $^2/_{23}$

E) $^1/_2$

This is a question on calculating basic probability. First of all, calculate how many items there are in total in the data set, which is also called the "sample space" or (S). Then reduce the data set if further items are removed. Probability can be expressed as a fraction. The number of items available in the total data set at the time of the draw goes in the denominator. The chance of the desired outcome, which is also referred to as the event or (E), goes in the numerator of the fraction. You can determine the chance of the event by calculating how many items are available in the subset of the desired outcome.

The correct answer is D.

You need to determine the amount of possible outcomes at the start of the day first of all.

The owner has 10 brown teddy bears, 8 white teddy bears, 4 black teddy bears, and 2 pink teddy bears when she opens the attraction at the start of the day. So, at the start of the day, she has 24 teddy bears: $10 + 8 + 4 + 2 = 24$

Then you need to reduce this amount by the quantity of items that have been removed. The problem tells us that she has given out a brown teddy bear, so there are 23 teddy bears left in the sample space: $24 - 1 = 23$

The event is the chance of the selection of a pink teddy bear. We know that there are two pink teddy bears left after the first prize winner receives his or her prize.

Finally, we need to put the event (the number representing the chance of the desired outcome) in the numerator and the number of possible remaining combinations (the sample space) in the denominator.

So the answer is $^2/_{23}$.

53) A magician pulls colored scarves out of a hat at random. The hat contains 5 red scarves and 6 blue scarves. The other scarves in the hat are green. If a scarf is pulled out of the hat at random, the probability that the scarf is red is $^1/_3$. How many green scarves are in the hat?

A) 3
B) 4
C) 5
D) 6
E) 7

> This question is asking you to determine the value missing from a sample space when calculating basic probability. This is like other problems on basic probability, but we need to work backwards to find the missing value. First, set up an equation to find the total items in the sample space. Then subtract the quantities of the known subsets from the total in order to determine the missing value.

The correct answer is B.

First, we will use variable T as the total number of items in the set. The probability of getting a red scarf is $^1/_3$.

So, set up an equation to find the total items in the data set.

$$\frac{5}{T} = \frac{1}{3}$$

$$\frac{5}{T} \times 3 = \frac{1}{3} \times 3$$

$$\frac{5}{T} \times 3 = 1$$

$$\frac{15}{T} = 1$$

$$\frac{15}{T} \times T = 1 \times T$$

$$15 = T$$

We have 5 red scarves, 6 blue scarves, and x green scarves in the data set that make up the total sample space, so now subtract the amount of red and blue scarves from the total in order to determine the number of green scarves.

$$5 + 6 + x = 15$$

$$11 + x = 15$$

$$11 - 11 + x = 15 - 11$$

$$x = 4$$

54) Becky rolls a fair pair of six-sided dice. One of the die is black and the other is red. Each die has values from 1 to 6. What is the probability that Becky will roll a 4 on the red die and a 5 on the black die?

A) $^1/_{36}$

B) $^2/_{36}$

C) $^1/_{12}$

D) $^2/_{12}$

E) $^{10}/_{12}$

This is an advanced problem on understanding probability models. For these questions, you will usually have two items, like two dice or a coin and a die. Each item will have various outcomes, like heads or tails for the coin or the different numbers on the die. To solve problems like this one, it is usually best to write out the possible outcomes in a list. This will help you visualize the number of possible outcomes that make up the sample space. Then circle or highlight the events from the list to get your answer.

The correct answer is A.

In this case, we have two items, each of which has a variable outcome. There are 6 numbers on the black die and 6 numbers on the red die.

Using multiplication, we can see that there are 36 possible combinations:

$6 \times 6 = 36$

To check your answer, you can list the possibilities of the various combinations:

(1,1)   (1,2)   (1,3)   (1,4)   (1,5)   (1,6)

(2,1)   (2,2)   (2,3)   (2,4)   (2,5)   (2,6)

(3,1)   (3,2)   (3,3)   (3,4)   (3,5)   (3,6)

(4,1)   (4,2)   (4,3)   (4,4)   (4,5)   (4,6)

(5,1)   (5,2)   (5,3)   **(5,4)**   (5,5)   (5,6)

(6,1)   (6,2)   (6,3)   (6,4)   (6,5)   (6,6)

If the number on the left in each set of parentheses represents the black die and the number on the right represents the red die, we can see that there is one chance that Becky will roll a 4 on the red die and a 5 on the black die.

The result is expressed as a fraction, with the event (chance of the desired outcome) in the numerator and the total sample space (total data set) in the denominator.

So, the answer is $1/36$.

55) The school board wants to poll a sample of students to get their opinions on dropping the music program in favor of having more sports programs. Which one of the following methods will result in the most statistically valid information about the opinions of all of the students at the high school?
A) To select ten students at random from each grade at the school
B) To speak to all of the members of the high school football team

C) To ask two members of each grade at random as they leave band practice

D) To give questionnaires out to the freshmen and sophomore students

E) To gather the opinions from students who are willing to speak to the school board

> This question is asking you about how best to use random sampling to draw conclusions about data. For information to be statistically valid, the data must be taken at random from a sample set of respondents that best represents the entire group.

The correct answer is A.

Our entire group in this problem is all of the students at the high school. So, it would be best to select ten students at random from each grade at the school.

The other answer choices would be biased in favor of members of certain groups, namely football players (answer B), band participants (answer C), younger students (answer D), and students who are not afraid to speak to the school board (answer E).

56) Which of the following are statistical questions? You may select more than one answer.

_____ (1) How long is that piece of string?

_____ (2) How many customers go to that coffee shop on Saturdays?

_____ (3) What time is algebra class?

_____ (4) What do students think about Mrs. Brown's calculus class?

_____ (5) What are the perimeter measurements of the high school parking lot?

> This question requires you to understand the difference between statistical and non-statistical questions. Statistical questions usually ask about opinions and behaviors. In addition, statistical questions will have a variety of different answers. On the other hand, questions about measuring time and distance are non-statistical questions because they have only one possible answer.

The correct answers are (2) and (4).

"How many customers go to that coffee shop on Saturdays?" is a statistical question because the amount of customers in the shop will vary from one weekend to the next.

"What do students think about Mrs. Brown's calculus class?" is also a statistical question because some students will have positive opinions, others will have negative opinions, and still others will have mixed opinions.

Praxis Core Practice Math Test 2

Number and Quantity Problems:

1) Which of the following is the greatest?
   A) 0.540
   B) 0.054
   C) 0.045
   D) 0.5045
   E) 0.0054

2) Which of the following is the most appropriate unit of measurement for the weight of a car?
   A) quarts
   B) horsepower
   C) gallons
   D) pounds per square inch
   E) tons

3) Farmer Brown has a field in which cows craze. He is going to buy fence panels to put up a fence along one side of the field. Each panel is 8 feet 6 inches long. He needs 11 panels to cover the entire side of the field. How long is the field?
   A) 60 feet 6 inches
   B) 72 feet 8 inches
   C) 93 feet 6 inches
   D) 102 feet 8 inches
   E) 110 feet 6 inches

4) In the Venn diagram below, circle A represents the integers from 3 to 13 inclusive, and circle B represents the integers 5 to 15 inclusive. How many integers are represented in region C of the diagram?

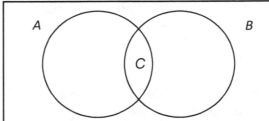

   A) 2
   B) 8
   C) 9
   D) 10
   E) 13

5) If the value of x is between 0.0007 and 0.0021, which of the following could be x?
   A) 0.0012
   B) 0.0006
   C) 0.0022
   D) 0.022
   E) 0.08

6) The total funds, represented by variable F, available for P charity projects is represented by the equation F = $500P + $3,700. If the charity has $40,000 available for projects, what is the greatest number of projects that can be completed?
   A) 72
   B) 73
   C) 74
   D) 79
   E) 80

7) The students at Lyndon High School have been asked about their plans to attend the Homecoming Dance. The chart below shows the responses of each grade level by percentages. Which figure below best approximates the percentage of the total number of students from all four grades who will attend the dance? Note that each grade level has roughly the same number of students.

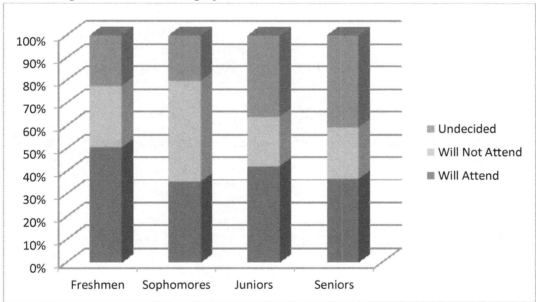

   A) 25%
   B) 35%
   C) 45%
   D) 55%
   E) 60%

8) Which of the following shows the numbers ordered from greatest to least?

A) $-\frac{1}{3}$, $\frac{1}{7}$, 1 , $\frac{1}{5}$

B) $-\frac{1}{3}$, $\frac{1}{5}$, $\frac{1}{7}$, 1

C) $-\frac{1}{3}$, 1 , $\frac{1}{7}$, $\frac{1}{5}$

D) 1 , $\frac{1}{5}$, $\frac{1}{7}$, $-\frac{1}{3}$

E) $-\frac{1}{3}$, $\frac{1}{7}$, $\frac{1}{5}$, 1

9) During each flight, a flight attendant must count the number of passengers on board the aircraft. The morning flight had 52 passengers more than the evening flight, and there were 540 passengers in total on the two flights that day. How many passengers were there on the evening flight?

A) 244

B) 296

C) 488

D) 540

E) 592

10) A cafeteria serves spaghetti to senior citizens on Fridays. The spaghetti comes prepared in large containers, and each container holds 15 servings of spaghetti. The cafeteria is expecting 82 senior citizens this Friday. What is the least number of containers of spaghetti that the cafeteria will need in order to serve all 82 people?

A)   4

B)   5

C)   6

D)   7

E)   15

11) A caterpillar travels 10.5 inches in 45 seconds. How far will it travel in 6 minutes?

A) 45 inches

B) 63 inches

C) 64 inches

D) 84 inches

E) 90 inches

12) Which one of the values will correctly satisfy the following mathematical statement: $\frac{2}{3} < ? < \frac{7}{9}$

A) $\frac{1}{3}$

B) $\frac{1}{5}$

C) $\frac{2}{6}$

D) $\frac{1}{2}$

E) $\frac{7}{10}$

13) Junab makes the following conversion:
10 gallons × 4 quarts / 1 gallon × 4 cups / 1 quart × 8 ounces / 1 cup
What conversion is he making?
A) Gallons to cups
B) Cups to gallons
C) Gallons to ounces
D) Ounces to gallons
E) Cups to quarts

14) Data on the number of vehicles involved in traffic accidents in Cedar Valley on certain dates is represented in the chart below.

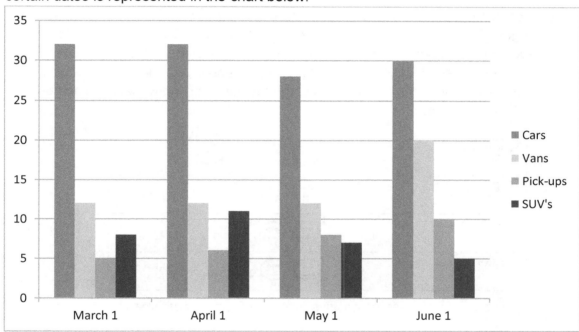

Pick-ups and vans were involved in approximately what percentage of total vehicle accidents on June 1?
A) 7.6%
B) 15%
C) 31%
D) 40%
E) 46%

15) A company is making its budget for the cost of employees to attend conferences for the year. It costs $7,500 per year in total for the company plus C dollars per employee. During the year, the company has E employees. If the company has budgeted $65,000 for conference attendance, which equation can be used to calculate the maximum cost per employee?

A) ($65,000 − $7,500) ÷ E
B) ($65,000 − $7,500) ÷ C
C) (C − $7,500) ÷ E
D) $65,000 ÷ E
E) ($65,000 ÷ E) − $7,500

16) The pictograph below illustrates the results of a customer satisfaction survey by region. Each of the four regions has one salesperson. Salespeople in each region receive bonuses based on the amount of positive customer feedback they receive. If the salespeople from all four regions received $540 in bonuses in total, how much bonus money does the company pay each individual salesperson per satisfied customer?

Region 1	☺ ☺ ☺ ☺
Region 2	☺ ☺ ☺
Region 3	☺ ☺
Region 4	☺ ☺ ☺

Each ☺ represents positive feedback from 10 customers.

A) $4.00
B) $4.50
C) $4.90
D) $5.00
E) $5.40

17) A megastore gives away a cell phone for free to any customer who spends
$2,250 or more in the store during the month of July. The store had $50,250 in
total sales income for July, and 310 customers made purchases in the store
during that month. Which equation below can be used to calculate the number of
free cell phones that the store gave away during the month of July?

A) ($50,250 ÷ $2,250)

B) ($50,250 ÷ 310)

C) ($50,250 ÷ $2,250) ÷ 310

D) ($50,250 − $2,250) ÷ 310

E) Cannot be determined from the information provided.

Algebra and Function Problems:

18) Which of the following is equivalent to the expression $2(x + 2)(x - 3)$ for all values of x?

A) $2x^2 - 2x - 12$
B) $2x^2 - 10x - 6$
C) $2x^2 + 2x - 12$
D) $2x^2 + 10x - 6$
E) $2x^2 - x - 3$

19) A plumber charges $100 per job, plus $25 per hour worked. He is going to do 5 jobs this month. He will earn a total of $4,000. How many hours will he work this month? Please write your answer in the space provided.

_____ hours this month

20) What are two possible values of x for the following equation? $x^2 + 6x + 8 = 0$

A) 1 and 2
B) 2 and 4
C) 6 and 8
D) −2 and −4
E) −3 and −4

21) Factor the following: $2xy - 6x^2y + 4x^2y^2$

A) $2xy(1 + 3x - 2xy)$
B) $2xy(1 - 3x + 2xy)$
C) $2xy(1 + 3x + 2xy)$
D) $2xy(1 - 3x - 2xy)$
E) $3xy(1 - 2x + 2xy)$

22) A is 3 times B, and B is 3 more than 6 times C. Which of the following describes the relationship between A and C?

A) A is 9 more than 18 times C.
B) A is 3 more than 3 times C.
C) A is 3 more than 18 times C.
D) A is 6 more than 3 times C.
E) A is 18 more than 9 times C.

23) The graph below shows the relationship between the number of days of rain per month and the amount of people who exercise outdoors per month. What relationship can be observed?

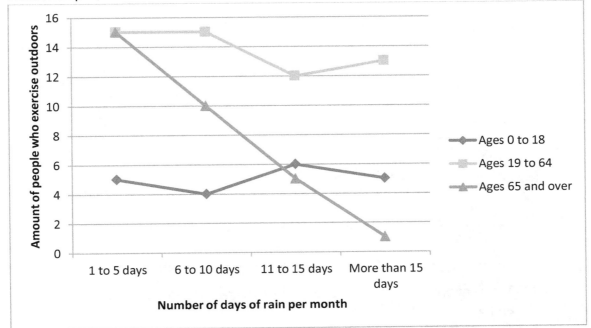

A) Young children are reliant upon an adult in order to exercise outdoors.
B) The exercise habits of working age people seem to fluctuate proportionately to the amount of rainfall.
C) In the 19 to 64 age group, there is a negative relationship between the number of days of rain and the amount of people who exercise outdoors.
D) People aged 65 and over seem less inclined to exercise outdoors when there is more rain.
E) No relationship can be observed because of the disparities inherent among the age groups.

24) Which of the following mathematical expressions equals $^3/_{xy}$?
A) $^3/_x \times {}^3/_y$
B) $3 \div 3xy$
C) $3 \div (xy)$
D) $^1/_3 \div 3xy$
E) $^1/_3 \div (x3y)$

25) Consider the scatterplot below and then choose the best answer from the options that follow.

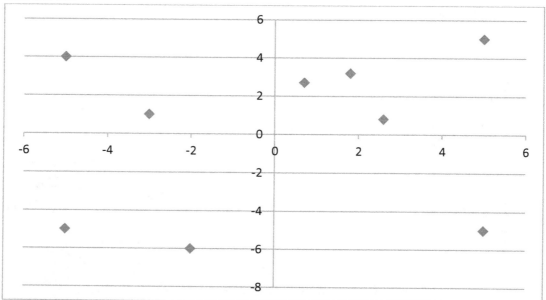

A) The scatterplot suggests a strong positive linear relationship between x and y.

B) The scatterplot suggests a strong negative linear relationship between x and y.

C) The scatterplot suggests a weak positive linear relationship between x and y.

D) The scatterplot suggests a weak negative linear relationship between x and y.

E) The scatterplot suggests that there is no relationship between x and y.

26) The graph of a line is shown on the xy plane below. The point that has the y-coordinate of 45 is not shown. What is the corresponding x-coordinate of that point?

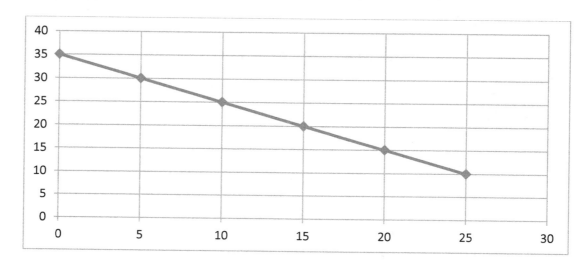

A) −10
B) −5
C) 0
D) 5
E) 30

27)

$$\frac{x^5}{x^2 - 6x} + \frac{5}{x} = ?$$

A)

$$\frac{4 + x^6}{x^2 - 3x}$$

B)

$$\frac{4x^2 - 16x}{x^7}$$

C)

$$\frac{x^5 + 5x + 30}{x^2 - 6x}$$

D)

$$\frac{x^5 + 5x - 30}{x^2 + 6x}$$

E)

$$\frac{x^5 + 5x - 30}{x^2 - 6x}$$

28) One-half inch on a map represents M miles. Which of the following equations represents $M + 5$ miles on the map?

A) $\frac{M+5}{2M}$

B) $\frac{0.5M+2.5}{M}$

C) $\frac{2M+5}{M}$

D) $\frac{M+5}{2}$

E) $\frac{1}{2}M + 5$

29)

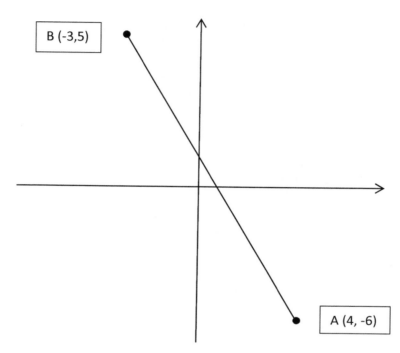

The line in the xy plane above is going to be shifted 2 units to the right and 3 units down. What are the coordinates of point A after the shift?
A) (6, –9)
B) (–1, 2)
C) (–5, 2)
D) (6, 0)
E) (2, 0)

30) The speed of a rocket is 25,000 miles per hour. How far does the rocket travel in 108,000 seconds?
A) 7.5×10^4 miles
B) 7.5×10^5 miles
C) 7.5×10^6 miles
D) 4.2×10^6 miles
E) 2.5×10^8 miles

31) $40 - \dfrac{3x}{5} \geq 10$, then $x \leq$?

A) 15

B) 30

C) 40

D) 50

E) 75

32) The number of visitors a museum had on Tuesday (T) was twice as much as the number of visitors it had on Monday (M). The number of visitors it had on Wednesday (W) was 20% greater than that on Tuesday. Which equation can be used to calculate the total number of visitors to the museum for the three days?
A) W + .20W + 2T + M
B) 2M + T + W
C) M + 1.2T + W
D) M + 2T + W
E) 5.4M

33) A construction company is building new homes on a housing development. It has an agreement with the municipality that H number of houses must be built every 30 days. If H number of houses are not built during the 30 day period, the company has to pay a penalty to the municipality of P dollars per house. The penalty is paid per house for the number of houses that fall short of the 30-day target. If A represents the actual number of houses built during the 30-day period, which equation below can be used to calculate the penalty for the 30-day period?
A) $(H - P) \times 30$
B) $(H - A) \times P$
C) $(A - H) \times 30$
D) $(A - H) \times P$
E) $(H - A) \times 30$

34) The graph of a line is shown on the *xy* plane below. The point that has the *x*-coordinate of 160 is not shown. What is the corresponding *y*-coordinate of that point?

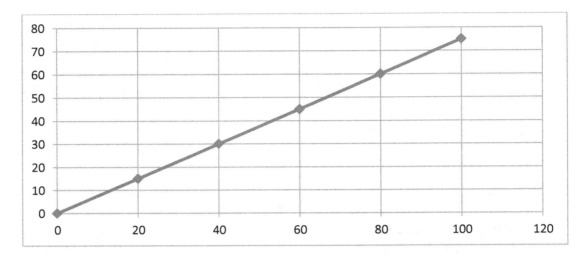

A) 115
B) 120
C) 125
D) 130
E) 135

Geometry Problems:

35) The central angle in the circle below measures 60° and is subtended by arc A which is 7π centimeters in length. How many centimeters long is the radius of this circle?

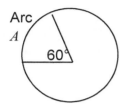

A) 42
B) 21
C) 6π
D) 6
E) 7

36) In the figure below, ∠Y is a right angle and ∠X = 60°.

If line segment YZ is 5 units long, then how long is line segment XY?

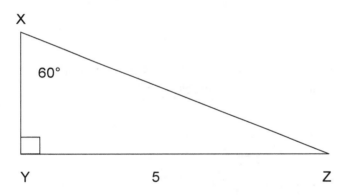

A) $\frac{5}{\sqrt{3}}$ units
B) 5 units
C) 6 units
D) 15 units
E) 30 units

37)   The figure in the *xy* plane below is going to be moved 7 units to the right and 6
        units down. What will the coordinates of point C be after the shift?

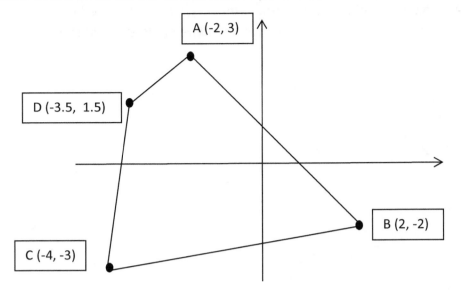

A (-2, 3)

D (-3.5, 1.5)

B (2, -2)

C (-4, -3)

A) (3, 3)
B) (9, –8)
C) (3, –9)
D) (–11, –9)
E) (–10, –10)

38)   Consider two concentric circles with radii of R_1 = 1 and R_2 = 2.4 as shown in the
        illustration below. Line *L* forms the diameter of the circles. What is the area of the
        lined part of the illustration?

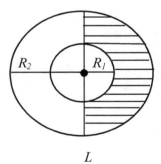

R_2 R_1

L

A) 0.7π
B) 1.4π
C) 2π
D) 2.38π
E) 2.8π

39) The line on the *xy*-graph below forms the diameter of the circle. What is the approximate circumference of the circle?

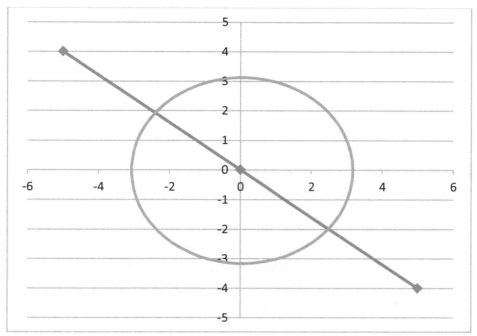

A) 3π
B) 6
C) 6π
D) 9
E) 9π

40) Mr. Lee is going to build a new garage. The garage will have a square base and a pyramid-shaped roof. The base measurement of the house is 20 feet. The height of the interior of the garage is 18 feet. The height of the roof from the center of its base to its peak is 15 feet. A diagram of the garage is shown below:

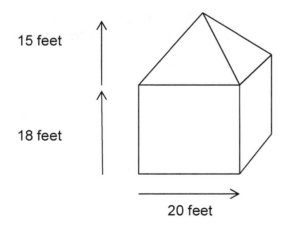

15 feet

18 feet

20 feet

What fraction expresses the ratio of the volume of the roof of the garage to the volume of the interior of the garage?

A) $5/6$

B) $5/18$

C) $1/4$

D) $3/4$

E) $4/7$

41) Which of the following statements about parallelograms is true? You may select more than one response.

_____ (1) A parallelogram has no right angles.

_____ (2) A parallelogram has opposite angles which are congruent.

_____ (3) A parallelogram has two pairs of parallel sides.

_____ (4) The opposite sides of a parallelogram are unequal in measure.

_____ (5) A rectangle is not a parallelogram.

42) Which of the following statements best describes supplementary angles?
A) Supplementary angles must add up to 90 degrees.
B) Supplementary angles must add up to 180 degrees.
C) Supplementary angles must add up to 360 degrees.
D) Supplementary angles must be congruent angles.
E) Supplementary angles must be opposite angles.

43) The area of a rectangle is 168 square units. This rectangle contains smaller rectangles that measure 2 square units each. How many of these small rectangles are needed to make up the entire rectangle?
A) 13
B) 28
C) 42
D) 84
E) 168

44) Acme Packaging uses string to secure their packages prior to shipment. The string is tied around the entire length and entire width of the package, as shown in the following illustration:

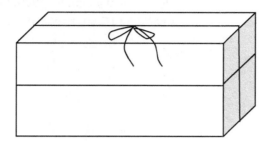

The box is ten inches in height, ten inches in depth, and twenty inches in length. An additional fifteen inches of string is needed to tie a bow on the top of the package. How much string is needed in total in order to tie up the entire package, including making the bow on the top?
A) 40
B) 80
C) 100
D) 120
E) 135

45) The triangle in the illustration below is an equilateral triangle. What is the measurement in degrees of angle a?

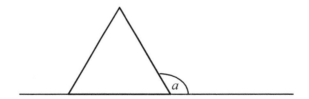

A) 40
B) 45
C) 60
D) 120
E) 130

Statistics and Probability Problems:

46) 110 students took a math test. The mean score for the 60 female students was 95, while the mean score for the 50 male students was 90. Which figure below best approximates the mean test score for all 110 students in the class?
A) 55
B) 90
C) 92.5
D) 92.73
E) 95

47) Carmen wanted to find the mean of the five tests she has taken this semester. However, she erroneously divided the total points from the five tests by 4, which gave her a result of 90. What is the correct mean of her five tests?
A) 72
B) 85
C) 86
D) 95
E) 112.5

48) Return on investment (ROI) percentages are provided for seven companies. The ROI will be negative if the company operated at a loss, but the ROI will be a positive value if the company operated at a profit. The ROI's for the seven companies were: –2%, 5%, 7.5%, 14%, 17%, 1.3%, –3%. Which figure below best approximates the mean ROI for the seven companies?
A) 2%
B) 5.7%
C) 6.25%
D) 7.5%
E) 20%

49) A group of families had the following household incomes on their tax returns: $65000, $52000, $125000, $89000, $36000, $84000, $31000, $135000, $74000, and $87000. What is the range?
A) 74000
B) 77800
C) 79000
D) 84000
E) 104000

50) In an athletic competition, the maximum possible amount of points was 25 points per participant. The scores for 15 different participants are displayed in the graph below. What was the median score for the 15 participants?

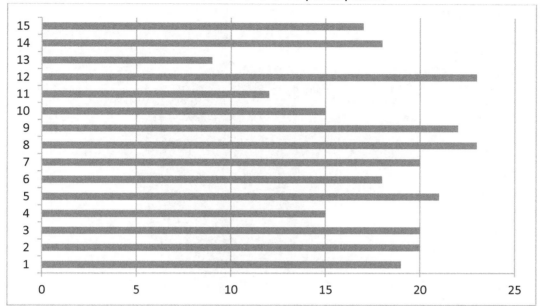

A) 8
B) 15
C) 17
D) 19
E) 23

51) A jar contains 4 red marbles, 6 green marbles, and 10 white marbles. If a marble is drawn from the jar at random, what is the probability that this marble is white?
A) $^{1}/_{2}$
B) $^{1}/_{5}$
C) $^{1}/_{10}$
D) $^{3}/_{10}$
E) $^{9}/_{20}$

52) Which of these numbers cannot be a probability? (There is more than one answer.)
A) −0.02
B) 0
C) 1.002
D) 1
E) $^{1}/_{4}$

53) An electricity company measures the energy consumption for each home in kilowatt hours (KWH). During July, the homes in one street had the levels of consumption in KWH in the chart show below. What is the mode of the level of energy consumption for this neighborhood for July?

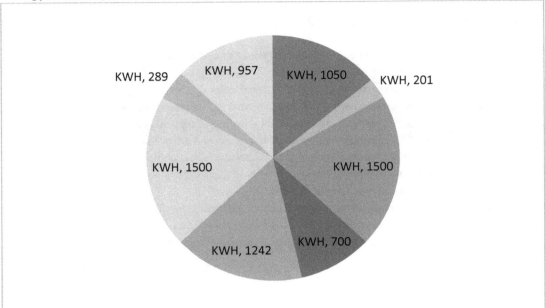

A) 700
B) 957
C) 828.5
D) 929.875
E) 1500

54) A die is rolled and a coin is tossed. What is the probability that the die shows an even number and the coin shows tails?

A) $^{1}/_{2}$
B) $^{1}/_{4}$
C) $^{1}/_{6}$
D) $^{1}/_{12}$
E) $^{1}/_{24}$

55) The blood types of 100 donors are shown in the following chart. If a donation from this group of donors is selected at random, what is the probability that type AB blood will be selected?

Blood Type	Number of donors
A positive	10
A negative	12
B positive	18
B negative	20
O type	25
AB type	15

A) $15/99$

B) $14/100$

C) $3/20$

D) $1/4$

E) $3/5$

56) A family is planning an annual picnic in Arizona. Rain is forecast for 45 days of the year, but when rain is forecast, the prediction is correct only 90% of the time. What is the probability that it will rain on the day of the picnic? Note that it is not a leap year.

A) 2.2222%

B) 11.0959%

C) 12.3288%

D) 45%

E) 90%

Praxis Core Practice Math Test 2 – Answer Key

1) A

2) E

3) C

4) C

5) A

6) A

7) B

8) D

9) A

10) C

11) D

12) E

13) C

14) E

15) A

16) B

17) E

18) A

19) 140 hours

20) D

21) B

22) A

23) D

24) C

25) E

26) A

27) E

28) B

29) A

30) B

31) D

32) E

33) B

34) B

35) B

36) A

37) C

38) D

39) C

40) B

41) (2) and (3)

42) B

43) D

44) E

45) D

46) D

47) A

48) B

49) E

50) D

51) A

52) A and C

53) E

54) B

55) C

56) B

Praxis Core Practice Math Test 2 – Solutions and Explanations

1) The correct answer is A. For problems with decimals, line the figures up in a column and add zeroes to fill in the column as shown below:

0.5400
0.0540
0.0450
0.5045
0.0054

If you still struggle with decimals, you can remove the decimal points and the zeroes before the other integers in order to see the answer more clearly.

~~0.~~5400
~~0.0~~540
~~0.0~~450
~~0.~~5045
~~0.00~~54

When we have removed the zeroes in front of the other numbers, we can see that the largest number is the first one, which is 0.54.

2) The correct answer is E. You will need to understand the basic concepts of United States' measurements for the exam. Remember that wet items are usually measured in pints and quarts, while dry items are usually measured in ounces and pounds, or tons in the case of extremely heavy quantities. Feet and inches are linear measurements; they are not used for weight. A gallon is a measurement of liquid substances. Horsepower measures the strength of an engine. Tons measure the weight of heavy items, so it would be a suitable unit of measurement for the weight of a car. Note that one ton is equal to two thousand pounds.

3) The correct answer is C. Each panel is 8 feet 6 inches long, and he needs 11 panels to cover the entire side of the field. So, we need to multiply 8 feet 6 inches by 11, and then simplify the result. Step 1: 8 feet × 11 = 88 feet; Step 2: 6 inches × 11 = 66 inches; Step 3: There are 12 inches in a foot, so we need to determine how many feet and inches there are in 66 inches. 66 inches ÷ 12 = 5 feet 6 inches; Step 4: Now add the two results together. 88 feet + 5 feet 6 inches = 93 feet 6 inches

4) The correct answer is C. Circle A contains these numbers: 3, 4, 5, 6, 7, 8, 9, 10, 11, 12, 13. Circle B contains these numbers: 5, 6, 7, 8, 9, 10, 11, 12, 13, 14, 15. Now look to see which numbers are included in both data sets for region C. 5, 6, 7, 8, 9, 10, 11, 12, 13 are included in both sets. So, region C contains 9 numbers.

5) The correct answer is A. This problem is like question 1 above, except here we need to find a missing value. Remember to put in zeroes and line up the decimal points when you compare the numbers.

```
    0.0007
A.  0.0012
B.  0.0006
C.  0.0022
D.  0.0220
E.  0.0800
    0.0021
```

Answer choice B is less than 0.0007, and answer choices C, D, and E are greater than 0.0021. Answer choice A (0.0012) is between 0.0007 and 0.0021, so it is the correct answer.

6) The correct answer is A. The equation is: F = $500P + $3,700. We are told that the total funds are $40,000 so put that in the equation to solve the problem.
$40,000 = $500P + $3,700
$40,000 – $3,700 = $500P
$36,300 = $500P
$36,300 ÷ 500 = $500 ÷ 500P
$36,300 ÷ 500 = 72.6
Since a fraction of a project cannot be undertaken, the greatest number of projects is 72.

7) The correct answer is B. The dark gray part at the bottom of each bar represents those students who will attend the dance. 45% of the freshman, 30% of the sophomores, 38% of the juniors, and 30% of the seniors will attend. Calculating the average, we get the overall percentage for all four grades: (45 + 30 + 38 + 30) ÷ 4 = 35.75%.   35% is the closest answer to 35.75%, so it best approximates our result.

8) The correct answer is D. To answer this type of question, you need these principles: (a) Positive numbers are greater than negative numbers; (b) When two fractions have the same numerator, the fraction with the smaller number in the denominator is the larger fraction. Accordingly, 1 is greater than $\frac{1}{5}$; $\frac{1}{5}$ is greater than $\frac{1}{7}$, and $\frac{1}{7}$ is greater than $-\frac{1}{3}$.

9) The correct answer is A. The problem tells us that the morning flight had 52 passengers more than the evening flight, and there were 540 passengers in total on the two flights that day. Step 1: First of all, we need to deduct the difference from the total: 540 – 52 = 488; In other words, there were 488 passengers on both flights combined, plus the 52 additional passengers on the morning flight. Step 2: Now divide this result by 2 to allocate an amount of passengers to each flight: 488 ÷ 2 = 244 passengers on the evening flight. Had the question asked you for the amount of passengers on the morning flight, you would have had to add back the amount of additional passengers to find the

Teaching Resources Center
Radford University

total amount of passengers for the morning flight: 244 + 52 = 296 passengers on the morning flight

10) The correct answer is C. Divide and then round up: 82 people in total ÷ 15 people served per container = 5.467 containers. We need to round up to 6 since we cannot purchase a fractional part of a container.

11) The correct answer is D. The question is asking us about a time duration of 6 minutes, so we need to calculate the amount of seconds in 6 minutes: 6 minutes × 60 seconds per minute = 360 seconds in total. Then divide the total time by the amount of time needed to make one journey: 360 seconds ÷ 45 seconds per journey = 8 journeys. Finally, multiply the number of journeys by the amount of inches per journey in order to get the total inches: 10.5 inches for 1 journey × 8 journeys = 84 inches in total

12) The correct answer is E. First of all, we need to find a common denominator for the fractions in the inequality, as well as for the fractions in the answer choices. In order to complete the problem quickly, you should not try to find the lowest common denominator, but just find any common denominator. We can do this by expressing all of the numbers with a denominator of 90, since 9 is the largest denominator in the equation and 10 is the largest denominator in the answer choices.

$^2/_3 \times {}^{30}/_{30} = {}^{60}/_{90}$
$^7/_9 \times {}^{10}/_{10} = {}^{70}/_{90}$

Then, express the original equation in terms of the common denominator: $^{60}/_{90} < ? < {}^{70}/_{90}$

Next, convert the answer choices to the common denominator.

A. $^1/_3 \times {}^{30}/_{30} = {}^{30}/_{90}$
B. $^1/_5 \times {}^{18}/_{18} = {}^{18}/_{90}$
C. $^2/_6 \times {}^{15}/_{15} = {}^{30}/_{90}$
D. $^1/_2 \times {}^{45}/_{45} = {}^{45}/_{90}$
E. $^7/_{10} \times {}^9/_9 = {}^{63}/_{90}$

Finally, compare the results to find the answer. By comparing the numerators (the top numbers of the fractions), we can see that $^{63}/_{90}$ lies between $^{60}/_{90}$ and $^{70}/_{90}$. So, E is the correct answer because $^{60}/_{90} < {}^{63}/_{90} < {}^{70}/_{90}$.

13) The correct answer is C. Look at the first item in the series and the numerator of last item in the series to find your answer:

10 **gallons** × 4 quarts / 1 gallon × 4 cups / 1 quart × 8 **ounces** / 1 cup

So, he is converting gallons to ounces.

14) The correct answer is E. Look at the bars for June 1 at the far right side of the graph. First, find the total amount of accidents on that date. Cars were involved in 30

accidents, vans in 20 accidents, pick-ups in 10 accidents, and SUV's in 5 accidents. So, there were 65 accidents in total (30 + 20 + 10 + 5 = 65). Then divide the number of accidents for pick-ups and vans into the total: 30 ÷ 65 = 46.1538% ≈ 46%

15) The correct answer is A. The total amount of the budget is $65,000. The up-front cost is $7,500, so we can determine the remaining amount of available funds by deducting the up-front cost from the total: $65,000 – $7,500. We have to divide the available amount by the number of employees (E) to get the maximum cost per employee: ($65,000 – $7,500) ÷ E

16) The correct answer is B. First of all, add up the amount of faces on the chart: 4 + 3 + 2 + 3 = 12 faces. Each face represents 10 customers, so multiply to get the total number of customers: 12 × 10 = 120 customers in total for all four regions. The salespeople received $540 in total, so we need to divide this by the amount of customers: $540 ÷ 120 customers = $4.50 per customer

17) The correct answer is E. We cannot determine the information because we would need to know exactly how much each individual customer spent in order to determine whether or not the particular customer received a free gift. We cannot simply divide and use the average.

18) The correct answer is A. The FOIL method is used on polynomials, which are equations that look like this: $(a + b)(c + d)$

You multiply the variables or terms in the parentheses in this order:
First **I**nside **O**utside **L**ast

We can use the FOIL method on our example equation as follows:
$(a + b)(c + d) =$
$(a \times c) + (a \times d) + (b \times c) + (b \times d) =$
$ac + ad + bc + bd$

You should use the FOIL method in this problem. Be very careful with the negative numbers when doing the multiplication.
$2(x + 2)(x - 3) =$
$2[(x \times x) + (x \times -3) + (2 \times x) + (2 \times -3)] =$
$2(x^2 + -3x + 2x + -6) =$
$2(x^2 - 3x + 2x - 6) =$
$2(x^2 - x - 6)$

Then multiply each term by the 2 at the front of the parentheses.
$2(x^2 - x - 6) =$
$2x^2 - 2x - 12$

19) The correct answer is 140 hours. The plumber is going to earn $4,000 for the month. He charges a set fee of $100 per job, and he will do 5 jobs, so we can calculate the total set fees first: $100 set fee per job × 5 jobs = $500 total set fees. Then deduct the set fees from the total for the month in order to determine the total for the hourly pay: $4,000 − $500 = $3,500. He earns $25 per hour, so divide the hourly rate into the total hourly pay in order to determine the number of hours he will work: $3,500 total hourly pay ÷ $25 per hour = 140 hours to work

20) The correct answer is D.

Step 1: Factor the equation.
$x^2 + 6x + 8 = 0$
$(x + 2)(x + 4) = 0$

Step 2: Now substitute 0 for x in the first pair of parentheses.
$(0 + 2)(x + 4) = 0$
$2(x + 4) = 0$
$2x + 8 = 0$
$2x + 8 - 8 = 0 - 8$
$2x = -8$
$2x \div 2 = -8 \div 2$
$x = -4$

Step 3: Then substitute 0 for x in the second pair of parentheses.
$(x + 2)(x + 4) = 0$
$(x + 2)(0 + 4) = 0$
$(x + 2)4 = 0$
$4x + 8 = 0$
$4x + 8 - 8 = 0 - 8$
$4x = -8$
$4x \div 4 = -8 \div 4$
$x = -2$

21) The correct answer is B. Any question that asks you to factor is simply another type of equivalent expression problem.

Looking at this equation, we can see that each term contains x. We can also see that each term contains y. So, first factor out xy.
$2xy - 6x^2y + 4x^2y^2 =$
$xy(2 - 6x + 4xy)$

Then, think about integers. We can see that all of the terms inside the parentheses are divisible by 2. Now let's factor out the 2. To do this, we divide each term inside the parentheses by 2.

$xy(2 - 6x + 4xy) =$
$2xy(1 - 3x + 2xy)$

22) The correct answer is A. The problem tells us that A is 3 times B, and B is 3 more than 6 times C. So, we need to create equations based on this information.
B is 3 more than 6 times C: B = 6C + 3
A is 3 times B: A = 3B
Since B = 6C + 3, we can substitute 6C + 3 for B in the second equation as follows:
A = 3B
A = 3(6C + 3)
A = 18C + 9
So, A is 9 more than 18 times C.

23) The correct answer is D. The most striking relationship on the graph is the line for ages 65 and over, which clearly shows a negative relationship between exercising outdoors and the number of days of rain per month. You will recall that a negative relationship exists when an increase in one variable causes a decrease in the other variable. So, we can conclude that people aged 65 and over seem less inclined to exercise outdoors when there is more rain.

24) The correct answer is C. The line in a fraction is the same as the division symbol. For example, $^a/_b = a \div b$. In the same way, $^3/_{xy} = 3 \div (xy)$.

25) The correct answer is E. When looking at scatterplots, try to see if the dots are roughly grouped into any kind of pattern or line. If so, positive or negative relationships may be represented. Here, however, the dots are located at what appear to be random places on all four quadrants of the graph. So, the scatterplot suggests that there is no relationship between x and y.

26) The correct answer is A. As x decreases by 5, y increases by 5. So, if we want to determine the x coordinate for $(x, 45)$ we need to deduct 10 from the x coordinate of $(0, 35)$. Therefore, the coordinates are $(-10, 45)$, and the answer is -10.

27) The correct answer is E. Find the lowest common denominator. Since x is common to both denominators, we can convert the denominator of the second fraction to the LCD by multiplying by $(x - 6)$.

$$\frac{x^5}{x^2 - 6x} + \frac{5}{x} =$$

$$\frac{x^5}{x^2 - 6x} + \left(\frac{5}{x} \times \frac{x - 6}{x - 6} \right) =$$

$$\frac{x^5}{x^2 - 6x} + \frac{5x - 30}{x^2 - 6x} =$$

$$\frac{x^5 + 5x - 30}{x^2 - 6x}$$

28) The correct answer is B. The ratio of 0.5 inch for *M* miles can be represented mathematically as $\frac{0.5}{M}$. The ratio for *M* + 5 is not known, so we can represent the unknown as x: $\frac{x}{M+5}$. Finally, use cross multiplication to solve the problem:

$$\frac{0.5}{M} = \frac{x}{M+5}$$

$$0.5 \times (M + 5) = Mx$$

Then divide by *M* to isolate x and solve the problem.

$$[0.5 \times (M + 5)] \div M = Mx \div M$$

$$\frac{0.5M + 2.5}{M} = x$$

29) The correct answer is A. Point A is (4, –6) at the start. The line is going to be shifted 2 units to the right (so we need to add 2 to the x coordinate) and 3 units down (so we need to subtract 3 from the y coordinate). So, the new position of point A will be (6, –9).

30) The correct answer is B. Convert the seconds to hours: 108,000 seconds ÷ 60 seconds per minute ÷ 60 minutes per hour = 30 hours. Then multiply by the speed of the rocket to get the miles: 25,000 miles per hour × 30 hours = 750,000 miles to travel. Finally, express your answer in exponential form: 750,000 = 7.5 × 100,000 = 7.5 × 10^5

31) The correct answer is D. Deal with the whole numbers on each side of the equation first.

$$40 - \frac{3x}{5} \geq 10$$

$$(40 - 40) - \frac{3x}{5} \geq 10 - 40$$

$$-\frac{3x}{5} \geq -30$$

Then deal with the fraction.

$$-\frac{3x}{5} \geq -30$$

$$\left(5 \times -\frac{3x}{5}\right) \geq -30 \times 5$$

$-3x \geq -30 \times 5$

$-3x \geq -150$

Then deal with the remaining whole numbers.

$-3x \geq -150$

$-3x \div 3 \geq -150 \div 3$

$-x \geq -150 \div 3$

$-x \geq -50$

Then deal with the negative number.

$-x \geq -50$

$-x + 50 \geq -50 + 50$

$-x + 50 \geq 0$

Finally, isolate the unknown variable as a positive number.

$-x + 50 \geq 0$

$-x + x + 50 \geq 0 + x$

$50 \geq x$

$x \leq 50$

32) The correct answer is E. Set up each part of the problem as an equation. The museum had twice as many visitors on Tuesday (T) as on Monday (M), so T = 2M. The number of visitors on Wednesday exceeded that of Tuesday by 20%, so W = 1.20 × T. Then express T in terms of M for Wednesday's visitors: W = 1.20 × T = 1.20 × 2M = 2.40M. Finally, add the amounts together for all three days: M + 2M + 2.40M = 5.4M

33) The correct answer is B. First, we need to calculate the shortage in the amount of houses actually built. If H represents the amount of houses that should be built and A represents the actual number of houses built, then the shortage is calculated as: $H - A$. The company has to pay P dollars per house for the shortage, so we calculate the total penalty by multiplying the shortage by the penalty per house: $(H - A) \times P$

34) The correct answer is B. We can see that when $x = 80$, $y = 60$. So, when $x = 160$, $y = 120$. Alternatively, if you prefer, you can determine that the line represents the function: $\int(x) = x \times 0.75$. Then substitute 160 for x: $x \times 0.75 = 160 \times 0.75 = 120$

35) The correct answer is B. Use the formula for circumference: $\pi \times$ radius $\times 2$. The angle given in the problem is 60°. If we divide the total 360° in the circle by the 60° angle, we have: 360 ÷ 60 = 6. So, there are 6 such arcs along this circle. We then have

to multiply the number of arcs by the length of each arc to get the circumference of the circle: $6 \times 7\pi = 42\pi$. Then, use the formula for the circumference of the circle to solve.

$42\pi = \pi \times 2 \times \text{radius}$
$42\pi \div 2 = \pi \times 2 \times \text{radius} \div 2$
$21\pi = \pi \times \text{radius}$
$21 = \text{radius}$

36) The correct answer is A. Triangle XYZ is a 30° - 60° - 90° triangle. As a result of the Pythagorean theorem, we know that its sides are in the ratio of $1 : \sqrt{3} : 2$. In other words, using relative measurements, the line segment opposite the 30° angle is 1 unit long, the line segment opposite the 60° angle is $\sqrt{3}$ units long, and the line segment opposite the right angle (the hypotenuse) is 2 units long. In this problem, line segment XY is opposite the 30° angle, so it is 1 proportional unit long. Line segment YZ is opposite the 60° angle, so it is $\sqrt{3}$ proportional units long. Line segment XZ (the hypotenuse) is the line opposite the right angle, so it is 2 proportional units long. So, in order to keep the measurements in proportion, we need to set up the following proportion: $XY/YZ = 1/\sqrt{3}$

Now substitute the known measurement of YZ from the above figure, which is 5 in this problem.

$$XY/YZ = 1/\sqrt{3}$$
$$\left(XY/5\right) = 1/\sqrt{3}$$
$$\left(XY/5 \times 5\right) = \left(1/\sqrt{3} \times 5\right)$$
$$XY = 5/\sqrt{3}$$

37) The correct answer is C. Before we shift the figure, point C has the coordinates (−4, −3). We are moving the figure 7 units to the right, thereby adding 7 to the x coordinate, and 6 units down, thereby subtracting 6 from the y coordinate. −4 + 7 = 3 and −3 − 6 = −9, so the new coordinates are: (3, −9).

38) The correct answer is D. The formula for the area of a circle is: $\pi \times R^2$. First, we need to calculate the area of the larger circle: $\pi \times 2.4^2 = 5.76\pi$. Then calculate the area of the smaller inner circle: $\pi \times 1^2 = \pi$. We need to find the difference between half of each circle, so divide the area of each circle by 2 and then subtract:

$$(5.76\pi \div 2) - (\pi \div 2) = \frac{5.76\pi}{2} - \frac{\pi}{2} = \frac{4.76\pi}{2} = 2.38\pi$$

39) The correct answer is C. The formula for circumference is: $\pi \times 2 \times R$. The center of the circle is on (0, 0) and the top edge of the circle extends to (0, 3), so the radius of the circle is 3. Therefore, the circumference is: $\pi \times 2 \times 3 = 6\pi$

40) The correct answer is B. The base of the garage is square, so its volume is calculated by taking the length times the width times the height: $20 \times 20 \times 18 = 7200$. The roof of the garage is a pyramid shape, so its volume is calculated by taking one-third of the base squared times the height: $(20 \times 20 \times 15) \times \frac{1}{3} = 6000 \div 3 = 2000$. So, the volume of the roof to the interior is: $\frac{2000}{7200} = \frac{5}{18}$

41) The correct answers are (2) and (3). A parallelogram is a four-sided figure that has two pairs of parallel sides. The opposite or facing sides of a parallelogram are of equal length and the opposite angles of a parallelogram are of equal measure. You will recall that congruent is another word for equal in measure. So, answers 2 and 3 are correct. A rectangle is a parallelogram with four angles of equal size (all of which are right angles), while a square is a parallelogram with four sides of equal length and four right angles.

42) The correct answer is B. Two angles are supplementary if they add up to 180 degrees.

43) The correct answer is D. A rectangle consisting of 2 square units will look like the following illustration: ⬚⬚

So, we divide the total number of squares in the larger rectangle by 2: $168 \div 2 = 84$

44) The correct answer is E. The string that goes around the front, back, and sides of the package is calculated as follows: 20 + 10 + 20 + 10 = 60. The string that goes around the top, bottom, and sides of the package is calculated in the same way since the top and bottom are equal in length to the front and back: 20 + 10 + 20 + 10 = 60. So, 120 inches of string is needed so far. Then, we need 15 extra inches for the bow: 120 + 15 = 135

45) The correct answer is D. An equilateral triangle has three equal sides and three equal angles. Since all 3 angles in any triangle need to add up to 180 degrees, each angle of an equilateral triangle is 60 degrees ($180 \div 3 = 60$). Angles that lie along the same side of a straight line must add up to 180. So, we calculate angle a as follows: 180 − 60 = 120

46) The correct answer is D. You need to find the total points for all the females and the total points for all the males: Females: 60 × 95 = 5700; Males: 50 × 90 = 4500. Then add these two amounts together and divide by the total number of students in the class to get your solution: (5700 + 4500) ÷ 110 = 10,200 ÷ 110 = 92.73 average for all 110 students

47) The correct answer is A. First you need to find the total points that the student earned. You do this by taking Carmen's erroneous average times 4: $4 \times 90 = 360$. Then divide the total points earned by the correct number of tests in order to get the correct average: $360 \div 5 = 72$

48) The correct answer is B. The mean is the arithmetic average. First, add up all of the items: $-2\% + 5\% + 7.5\% + 14\% + 17\% + 1.3\% + -3\% = 39.8\%$. Then divide by 7 since there are 7 companies in the set: $39.8\% \div 7 = 5.68\% \approx 5.7\%$

49) The correct answer is E. The range is the highest number minus the lowest number. Our data set is: $65000, $52000, $125000, $89000, $36000, $84000, $31000, $135000, $74000, and $87000. So, the range is: $135000 - $31000 = $104000

50) The correct answer is D. The median is the number that is halfway through the set. Our data set is: 19, 20, 20, 15, 21, 18, 20, 23, 22, 15, 12, 23, 9, 18, 17. First, put the numbers in ascending order: 9, 12, 15, 15, 17, 18, 18, 19, 20, 20, 20, 21, 22, 23, 23. We have 15 numbers, so the 8th number in the set is halfway and is therefore the median: 9, 12, 15, 15, 17, 18, 18, **19**, 20, 20, 20, 21, 22, 23, 23

51) The correct answer is A. Your first step is to calculate the total amount of items in the data set: 4 red marbles + 6 green marbles + 10 white marbles = 20 marbles in total. The probability is expressed with the subset in the numerator and the total remaining data set in the denominator. So, the chance of drawing a white marble is $^{10}/_{20} = ^{1}/_{2}$

52) The correct answers are A and C. Probability will be 1 for a 100% probability, 0 for something that has no change of occurring, or a positive number less than 1 for all other probabilities. Probability can be expressed as a decimal or a fraction. Probability therefore cannot be a negative number or a number greater than 1.

53) The correct answer is E. The mode is the number in the set that occurs most frequently. Our data set is: 1050, 201, 1500, 700, 1242, 1500, 289, 957. The number 1500 is the only number that occurs more than once, so it is the mode.

54) The correct answer is B. The data set can be expressed as follows:
(1,H),(2,H),(3,H),(4,H),(5,H),(6,H), (1,T),(2,T),(3,T),(4,T),(5,T),(6,T)
Counting the items in the above set, we can see that there are 12 items in total.
The desired outcome is that the die shows an even number and the coin shows a tails.
The possible outcomes are: {(2,T),(4,T),(6,T)}
So, the probability is: $^{3}/_{12} = ^{1}/_{4}$

55) The correct answer is C. The total for the data set is: $10 + 12 + 18 + 20 + 25 + 15 = 100$. There are 15 donors with type AB blood, so the probability is $^{15}/_{100} = ^{3}/_{20}$

56) The correct answer is B. The event is defined as the chance of rain. In terms of probabilities, we know that there are 365 days in non-leap years, so this goes in the denominator. The chance of rain goes in the numerator: $^{45}/_{365} = 12.3288\%$. However, the forecast is correct only 90% of the time: $12.3288\% \times 90\% = 11.0959\%$

Praxis Core Practice Math Test 3

Number and Quantity Problems:

1) Pilar does the following calculation:

10 kilometers × 1000 meters/1 kilometer × 100 centimeters/1 meter

What conversion is she doing?

A) Meters to kilometers
B) Centimeters to meters
C) Kilometers to meters
D) Kilometers to centimeters
E) Centimeters to kilometers

2) Which of the following shows the numbers ordered from least to greatest?

A) 0.2135
0.3152
0.0253
0.0012

B) 0.3152
0.2135
0.0253
0.0012

C) 0.0253
0.0012
0.3152
0.2135

D) 0.0012
0.0253
0.2135
0.3152

E) 0.3152
0.2135
0.0012
0.0253

3) If $\frac{x}{24}$ is between 8 and 9, which of the following could be the value of x?

A) 190
B) 191
C) 200
D) 217
E) 220

4) The ratio of bags of apples to bags of oranges in a particular grocery store is 2 to 3. If there are 44 bags of apples in the store, how many bags of oranges are there?
   A) 33
   B) 48
   C) 55
   D) 63
   E) 66

5) Ali uses a jar of coffee every 7 days. At least how many jars of coffee will he need to last the entire year?
   A) 48
   B) 50
   C) 52
   D) 53
   E) 54

6) At the beginning of class, $1/5$ of the students leave to go to singing lessons. Then $1/4$ of the remaining students leave to go to the principal's office. If 18 students are then left in the class, how many students were there at the beginning of class?
   A) 90
   B) 45
   C) 30
   D) 25
   E) 24

7) In the last step of doing a calculation, Wei Li added 92 instead of subtracting 92. What shortcut can Wei Li perform in order to get the correct calculation?
   A) Subtract 46 from his erroneous result.
   B) Add 92 to his erroneous result.
   C) Subtract 92 from his erroneous result.
   D) Add 184 to his erroneous result.
   E) Subtract 184 from his erroneous result.

8) Which of the following units of measure is most likely to be the approximate width of a tennis court?
   A) 10 meters
   B) 100 yards
   C) 3000 inches
   D) 3600 centimeters
   E) $1/4$ mile

9) A dance academy had 300 students at the beginning of January. It lost 5% of its students during the month. However, 15 new students joined the academy on the last day of the month. If this pattern continues for the next two months, how many students will there be at the academy at the end of March?
    A) 285
    B) 300
    C) 310
    D) 315
    E) 320

10) In a group of children, one-half have had a tetanus shot. Of that half, only one-third suffered wounds that would have caused tetanus. In which of the following graphs does the dark gray area represent that third of the group?

A)

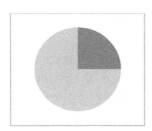

B)

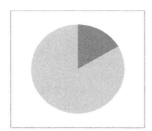

C)

D)

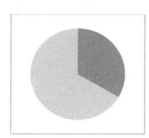

E)

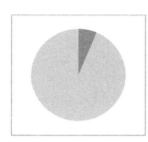

11) The residents of Hendersonville took a census. As part of the census, each resident had to indicate how many relatives they had living within a ten-mile radius of the town. The results of that particular question on the census are represented in the graph below.

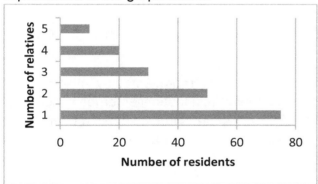

How many residents of Hendersonville had more than 3 relatives living within a ten-mile radius of the town?

A) 10
B) 20
C) 30
D) 155
E) 175

12) The price of a wool coat is reduced 12.5% at the end of the winter. If the original price of the coat was $120, what will the price be after the reduction?
A) $108.00
B) $107.50
C) $105.70
D) $105.00
E) $100.00

13) A motorcycle traveled 38.4 miles in $^4/_5$ of an hour. What was the speed of the motorcycle in miles per hour?
A) 9.6
B) 30.72
C) 48
D) 52
E) 60

14) A factory that makes microchips produces 20 times as many functioning chips as defective chips. If the factory produced 11,235 chips in total last week, how many of them were defective?
A) 535
B) 561
C) 1,070
D) 10,700
E) 11,215

15) A town has recently suffered a flood. The total cost, represented by variable C, which is available to accommodate R number of residents in emergency housing is represented by the equation C = $750R + $2,550. If the town has a total of $55,000 available for emergency housing, what is the greatest number of residents that it can house?
A) 68
B) 69
C) 70
D) 71
E) 75

16) The numbers in the following list are ordered from least to greatest:
$$\alpha, \ ^2/_7, \ ^8/_9, \ 1.35, \ ^{11}/_3, \ \mu$$
Which of the following could be the value of μ? Be sure to choose all possible answers.
A) 3.5
B) $^{10}/_4$
C) 4.1

D) $^{1}/_{6}$

E) $^{3}/_{7}$

17) The pictograph below shows the number of traffic violations that occur every week in a certain city. The fine for speeding violations is $50 per violation. The fine for other violations is $20 per violation. The total collected for all three types of violations was $6,000. What is the fine for each parking violation?

Speeding	✧ ✧
Parking	✧
Other violations	✧ ✧ ✧

Each ✧ represents 30 violations.

A) $20

B) $30

C) $40

D) $100

E) $140

Algebra and Function Problems:

18) $(x^2 - x - 6) \div (x - 3) = ?$
   A) 2x
   B) x − 2
   C) x − 2
   D) y + 2
   E) x + 2

19) Perform the operation: $(5ab - 6a)(3ab^3 - 4b^2 - 3a)$
   A) $15a^2b^4 - 20ab^3 - 15a^2b - 18a^2b^3 - 24ab^2 - 18a^2$
   B) $15a^2b^4 - 20ab^3 - 15a^2b - 18a^2b^3 + 24ab^2 + 18a^2$
   C) $15a^2b^4 - 20ab^3 - 15a^2b - 18a^2b^3 - 24ab^2 + 18a^2$
   D) $15ab^4 - 20ab^3 - 15a^2b - 18a^2b^3 + 24ab^2 + 18a^2$
   E) $-15a^2b^4 - 20ab^3 - 15a^2b - 18a^2b^3 + 24ab^2 + 18a^2$

20) If $4(2x + 2) = 6(x - 1) + 21$, what is the value of x?

   State your answer as a fraction in the spaces provided.

   Numerator value of x = _____

   Denominator value of x = _____

21) The price of a sofa at a local furniture store was x dollars on Wednesday this week. On Thursday, the price of the sofa was reduced by 10% of Wednesday's price. On Friday, the price of the sofa was reduced again by 15% of Thursday's price. Which of the following expressions can be used to calculate the price of the sofa on Friday?
   A) $(0.25)\,x$
   B) $(0.75)\,x$
   C) $(0.10)(0.15)\,x$
   D) $(0.10)(0.85)\,x$
   E) $(0.90)(0.85)\,x$

22) If $2x + y = 6$ and $m - n = 2$, what is the value of $(4x + 2y)(4m - 4n)$?
   A) 8
   B) 12
   C) 16

D) 72

E) 96

23) There are three boys in a family, named Alex, Burt, and Zander. Alex is twice as old as Burt, and Burt is one year older than three times the age of Zander. Which of the following statements best describes the relationship between the ages of the boys?

A) Alex is 4 years older than 6 times the age of Zander.

B) Alex is 2 years older than 6 times the age of Zander.

C) Alex is 4 years older than 3 times the age of Zander.

D) Alex is 2 years older than 3 times the age of Zander.

E) Alex is 1 year older than 6 times the age of Zander.

24) $\dfrac{x + \dfrac{1}{5}}{\dfrac{1}{x}} = ?$

A) $x^2 + 5$

B) $\dfrac{x^3}{5}$

C) $x^2 + \dfrac{x}{5}$

D) $\dfrac{x + \dfrac{1}{5}}{x}$

E) $\dfrac{x}{x + \dfrac{1}{5}}$

25) If $\frac{1}{5}x + 3 = 5$, then $x = ?$

A) $\frac{8}{5}$

B) $-\frac{8}{5}$

C) 8

D) 10

E) −10

26) The graph of a linear equation is shown below. Which one of the tables of values best represents the points on the graph?

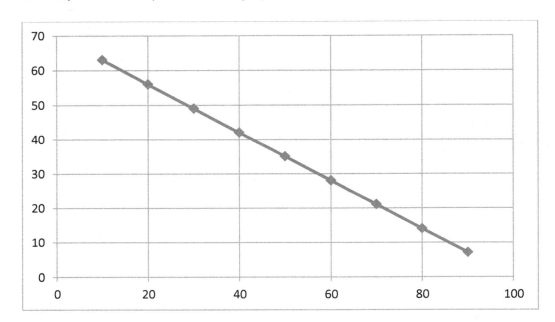

A)

x	y
5	65
10	64
15	63
20	62

B)

x	y
5	68
15	60
25	52
35	54

C)

x	y
10	63
20	56
30	49
40	42

D)

x	y
10	68
20	60
30	52
40	44

E)

x	y
30	42
40	35
50	28
60	21

27) An athlete ran 10 miles in 1.5 hours. The graph below shows the miles the athlete ran every 10 minutes. According to the graph, how many miles did the athlete run in the first 30 minutes?

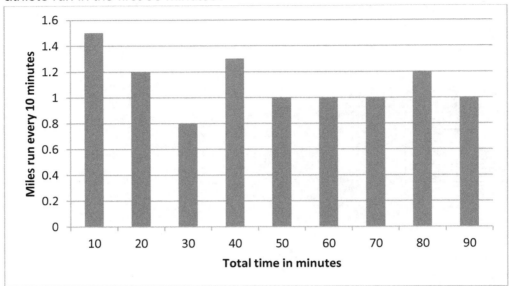

A) 0.8 miles
B) 2.0 miles
C) 3.0 miles
D) 3.4 miles
E) 3.5 miles

28) Which of the following steps will solve the equation for x: $18 = 3(x + 5)$
A) Subtract 5 from each side of the equation, and then divide both sides by 3.
B) Subtract 18 from each side of the equation, and then divide both sides by 5.
C) Multiply both x and 5 by 3 on the right side of the equation. Then subtract 15 from each side of the equation.
D) Divide each side of the equation by 3. Then subtract 5 from both sides of the equation.
E) Divide each side of the equation by 5. Then subtract 3 from both sides of the equation.

29) Factor the following. Then simplify. $\dfrac{x^2 + 5x + 6}{x^2 + 6x + 8} \times \dfrac{x^2 + 4x}{x^2 + 8x + 15}$

A)

$$\dfrac{5}{x + 5}$$

B)

$$\frac{x}{x+5}$$

C)

$$\frac{x+3}{x+4}$$

D)

$$\frac{x+4}{x+3}$$

E)

$$\frac{x^2}{x^2+8x}$$

30) A clothing store sells jackets and jeans at a discount during a sales period. T represents the number of jackets sold and N represents the number of jeans sold. The total amount of money the store collected for sales of jeans and jackets during the sales period was $4,000. The amount of money earned from selling jackets was one-third of that earned from selling jeans. The jeans sold for $20 a pair. How many pairs of jeans did the store sell during the sales period?
   A)   15
   B)   20
   C)   150
   D)   200
   E) 3000

31) If Д is a special operation defined by $(x \ Д \ y) = (5x \div 4y)$ and $(8 \ Д \ y) = 5$, then $y = ?$
   A)   2
   B)   4
   C)   16
   D) 0.25
   E) 0.50

32) Which of the following is equivalent to the expression $36 - 2x$ for all values of x?

A) $6 + 2(15 - x)$

B) $6(6 - 2x)$

C) $39 - (3 - 2x)$

D) $8(5 - 2x) - 4$

E) $6(6 - 4x) - 2x$

33) Carlos is going to buy a house. The total purchase price of the house is represented by variable H. He will pay D dollars immediately, and then he will make equal payments (P) each month for M months. If H = \$300,000, P = \$700 and M = 360, how much will Carlos pay immediately?

A) \$38,000

B) \$48,000

C) \$58,000

D) \$252,000

E) \$299,300

34) Which of the following equations is equivalent to $\frac{x}{5} \div \frac{9}{y}$?

A) $\frac{xy}{45}$

B) $\frac{9x}{5y}$

C) $\frac{1}{9} \times \frac{x}{5y}$

D) $\frac{1}{5} \times \frac{9}{5y}$

E) $\frac{1}{5} \div \frac{9x}{y}$

Geometry Problems:

35) The radius (R) of circle A is 5 centimeters. The radius of circle B is 3 centimeters. Which of the following statements is true? You may select more than 1 answer.

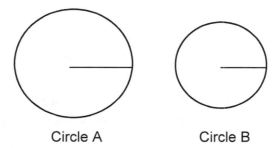

Circle A   Circle B

A) The difference between the areas of the circles is 2.
B) The difference between the areas of the circles is 9π.
C) The difference between the circumferences of the circles is 2.
D) The difference between the circumferences of the circles is 4π.
E) The difference between the diameters of the circles is 4.

36) Liz wants to put new vinyl flooring in her kitchen. She will buy the flooring in square pieces that measure 1 square foot each. The entire room is 8 feet by 12 feet. The cupboards are two feet deep from front to back. Flooring will not be put under the cupboards. A diagram of her kitchen is provided.

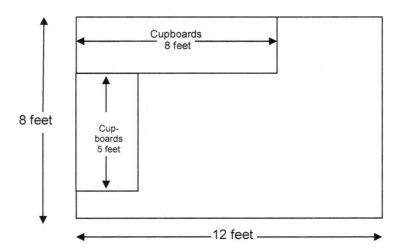

How many pieces of vinyl will Liz need to cover her floor?
A) 120
B) 96
C) 70
D) 84
E) 88

37) A large wheel (L) has a radius of 10 inches. A small wheel (S) has a radius of 6 inches. If the large wheel is going to travel 360 revolutions, how many more revolutions does the small wheel need to make to cover the same distance?
A) 120
B) 240
C) 360
D) 720
E) 120π

38) Consider the vertex of an angle at the center of a circle. The diameter of the circle is 2. If the angle measures 90 degrees, what is the arc length relating to the angle?
A) $\pi/2$
B) $\pi/4$
C) 2π
D) 4π
E) 8π

39) A farmer has a rectangular pen in which he keeps animals. He has decided to divide the pen into two parts. To divide the pen, he will erect a fence diagonally from the two corners, as shown in the diagram below. How long in yards is the diagonal fence?

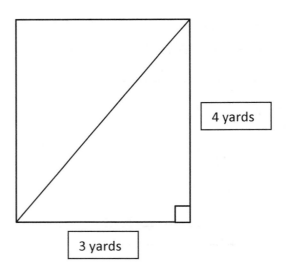

4 yards

3 yards

A) 4
B) 5
C) 5.5
D) 6
E) 6.5

40) The diagram below shows a figure made from a semicircle, a rectangle, and an equilateral triangle. The rectangle has a length of 18 inches and a width of 10 inches. What is the perimeter of the figure?

A) 56 inches + 5π inches
B) 56 inches + 10π inches
C) 56 inches + 12.5π inches
D) 56 inches + 25π inches
E) 208.9 inches + 12.5π inches

41) The illustration below shows a pyramid with a base width of 3, a base length of 5, and a volume of 30. What is the height of the pyramid?

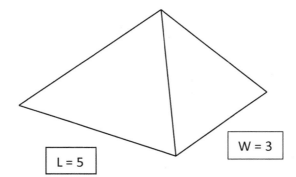

W = 3

L = 5

A) 2
B) 3
C) 5
D) 6
E) 7

42) What is the area of the figure below?

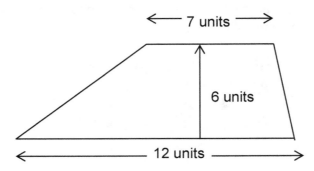

A) 57
B) 72
C) 84
D) 202
E) 252

43) The illustration below shows a pentagon. The shaded part at the top of the pentagon has a height of 6 inches.

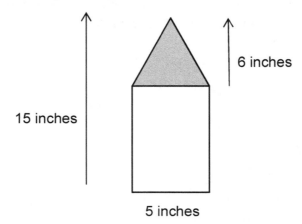

The height of the entire pentagon is 15 inches, and the base of the pentagon is 5 inches. What fraction expresses the area of the shaded part to the area of the entire pentagon? State your answer as a simplified fraction in the spaces provided.

Numerator value = _____

Denominator value = _____

44) A right triangle has two sides which have respective lengths of 5 and 3. The other side of the triangle is side x. Which of the following values could be the length of side x? You may select more than one answer.

_____ $\sqrt{28}$

_____ $\sqrt{34}$

_____ 2

_____ 4

_____ 6

45) In the figure below, x and y are parallel lines, and line z is a transversal crossing both x and y. Which three angles are equal in measure? You may select more than one answer.

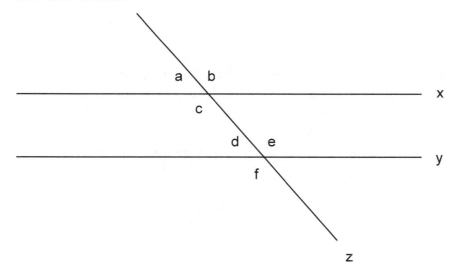

A) $\angle a, \angle b, \angle c$
B) $\angle b, \angle c, \angle f$
C) $\angle b, \angle e, \angle f$
D) $\angle a, \angle d, \angle e$
E) $\angle a, \angle d, \angle f$

Statistics and Probability Problems:

46)   What is the median of the numbers in the following list?:

2.5, 9.4, 3.1, 1.7, 3.2, 8.2, 4.5, 6.4, 7.8

A) 3.2
B) 4.5
C) 5.2
D) 6.4
E) 7.7

47)   Suki rolls a fair pair of six-sided dice. Each die has values from 1 to 6. She rolls an even number on her first roll. What is the probability that she will roll an odd number on her next roll?

A) $1/2$
B) $1/6$
C) $2/6$
D) $6/11$
E) $5/11$

48)   The state highway department wants to find out how the residents of Buford feel about a new road being constructed around their town. Which one of the following methods will result in the most statistically valid information about the opinions of the residents at the town?
A) To question drivers of a random selection of vehicles traveling through Buford
B) To poll drivers at random as they exit the interstate highway near Buford
C) To ask car owners living in Buford to participate in a survey
D) To select a random sample of names from Buford's voting register
E) To select participants for a survey from a list of all of the citizens living in Buford

49)   A student receives the following scores on his exams during the semester:
89, 65, 75, 68, 82, 74, 86
What is the mean of his scores?
A) 24
B) 74
C) 75
D) 77
E) 82

50) A clown pulls balloons out of a bag at random to blow up and give to children during a birthday party. At the start of the party, there are 10 red balloons, 7 green balloons, 6 purple balloons, 5 orange balloons, and 11 blue balloons in the bag. The clown selects the first balloon, which is blue, and gives it to the first child. If the second child gets an orange balloon, what is the probability that the third child will get a blue balloon?

A) $^{11}/_{37}$

B) $^{10}/_{37}$

C) $^{11}/_{39}$

D) $^{10}/_{39}$

E) $^{1}/_{11}$

51) What is the mode of the numbers in the following list?

$$1.6, 2.9, 4.5, 2.5, 2.5, 5.1, 5.4$$

A) 3.5

B) 3.1

C) 3.0

D) 2.9

E) 2.5

52) Which of the following graphs represents five values for which the median of the values equals the mean of the values?

A)

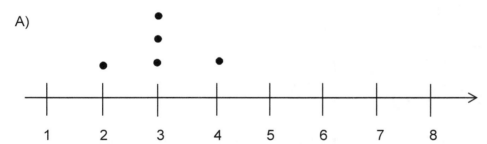

B)

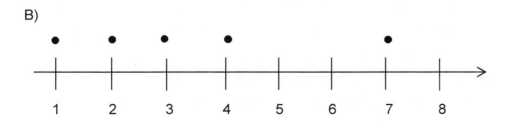

C)

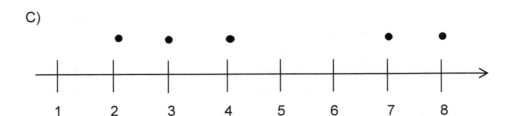

D)

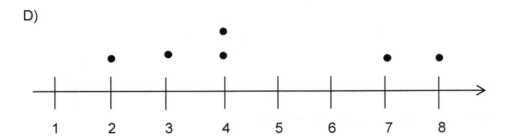

E)

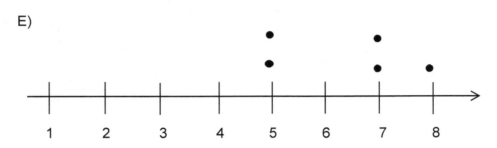

53) There are 10 cars in a parking lot. Nine of the cars are 2, 3, 4, 5, 6, 7, 9, 10, and 12 years old, respectively. If the average age of the 10 cars is 6 years old, how old is the 10th car?

A) 1 year old
B) 2 years old
C) 3 years old
D) 4 years old
E) 5 years old

54) Which of the following are statistical questions? You may select more than one answer.

_____ (1) What size shoe does Mrs. Shapiro wear?

_____ (2) How many residents of the town oppose the tax increase?

_____ (3) Will it rain tomorrow?

_____ (4) How many miles can that car travel on a tank of gasoline?

_____ (5) Do most college graduates in our state find jobs within one year of

leaving college?

55) The range and mean of 5 numbers are 10 and 14 respectively. The five numbers are positive integers greater than 0. If the range is increased by 2, which of the following could be true of the numbers in the new set? You may select more than one answer.

A) The highest number is increased by 2.

B) The highest number is increased by 1 and the lowest number is decreased by 1.

C) The highest number is decreased by 1 and the lowest number is increased by 1.

D) The lowest number is increased by 2.

E) The mean of the numbers remains unchanged

56) A deck of cards contains 13 hearts, 13 diamonds, 13 clubs, and 13 spades. Cards are selected from the deck at random. Once selected, the cards are discarded and are not placed back into the deck. Two spades, one heart, and a club are drawn from the deck. What is the probability that the next card drawn from the deck will be a heart?

A) $^1/_{13}$

B) $^1/_{12}$

C) $^{13}/_{52}$

D) $^{13}/_{48}$

E) $^1/_4$

Praxis Core Practice Math Test 3 – Answer Key

1) D

2) D

3) C

4) E

5) C

6) C

7) E

8) A

9) B

10) B

11) C

12) D

13) C

14) A

15) B

16) C

17) C

18) E

19) B

20) numerator value = 7; denominator value = 2

21) E

22) E

23) B

24) C

25) D

26) C

27) E

28) D

29) B

30) C

31) A

32) A

33) B

34) A

35) D and E

36) C

37) B

38) A

39) B

40) A

41) D

42) A

43) numerator value = 1; denominator value = 4

44) $\sqrt{34}$ and 4

45) B and C

46) B

47) A

48) E

49) D

50) B

51) E

52) A

53) B

54) 2 and 5

55) A and B

56) E

Praxis Core Practice Math Test 3 – Solutions and Explanations

1) The correct answer is D. Remember to look at the first item in the series, as well as the numerator of the final item in the series in order to understand the conversion:
10 **kilometers** × 1000 meters/1 kilometer × 100 **centimeters**/1 meter
In other words, she is converting kilometers to centimeters.

2) The correct answer is D. We have the following numbers in our problem:

0.0012
0.0253
0.2135
0.3152

If you still do not feel confident with decimals, remember that you can remove the decimal point and the zeroes after the decimal but before the other integers in order to see the answer more clearly.

   12
  253
2135
3152

3) The correct answer is C. If $\frac{x}{24}$ is between 8 and 9, x will need to be between 192 and 216, since $\frac{192}{24}$ = 192 ÷ 24 = 8 and $\frac{216}{24}$ = 216 ÷ 24 = 9. 200 is the only number from the answer choices that is greater than 192 and less than 216.

4) The correct answer is E. The ratio of bags of apples to bags of oranges is 2 to 3, so for every two bags of apples, there are three bags of oranges. First, take the total amount of bags of apples and divide by 2: 44 ÷ 2 = 22. Then multiply this by 3 to determine how many bags of oranges are in the store: 22 × 3 = 66.

5) The correct answer is C. If Ali uses a jar of coffee every week, he needs 52 jars to last a year since there are 52 weeks in a year.

6) The correct answer is C. Work backwards based on the facts given. There are 18 students left at the end after one-fourth of them left for the principal's office. So, set up an equation for this:
18 + $^1/_4$T = T
18 + $^1/_4$T − $^1/_4$T = T − $^1/_4$T
18 = $^3/_4$T
18 × 4 = $^3/_4$T × 4
72 = 3T
72 ÷ 3 = 3T ÷ 3
24 = T

So, before the group of pupils left to see the principal, there were 24 students in the class. We know that one-fifth of the students left at the beginning to go to singing lessons, so we need to set up an equation for this:

$24 + \frac{1}{5}T = T$

$24 + \frac{1}{5}T - \frac{1}{5}T = T - \frac{1}{5}T$

$24 = \frac{4}{5}T$

$24 \times 5 = \frac{4}{5}T \times 5$

$120 = 4T$

$120 \div 4 = 4T \div 4$

$30 = T$

7) The correct answer is E. He needs to subtract the 92 that he added by mistake to get back to his starting point. Then he needs to subtract 92 again to get the correct result. So, he can subtract 92 two times or simply shortcut by subtracting 184 (82 × 82 = 194).

8) The correct answer is A. Tennis courts measure approximately 36 feet in width by 78 feet in length. Ten meters is approximately 33 feet.

9) The correct answer is B. At the beginning of January, there are 300 students, but 5% of the students leave during the month, so we have 95% left at the end of the month: 300 × 95% = 285. Then 15 students join on the last day of the month, so we add that back in to get to the total at the end of January: 285 + 15 = 300. If this pattern continues, there will always be 300 students in the academy at the end of any month.

10) The correct answer is B. The question is asking us to calculate one third of one half. So, we multiply to get our answer: $\frac{1}{2} \times \frac{1}{3} = \frac{(1 \times 1)}{(2 \times 3)} = \frac{1}{6}$

11) The correct answer is C. The question is asking us how many residents have more than 3 relatives nearby, so we need to add the bars for 4 and 5 relatives from the chart. 20 residents have 4 relatives nearby and 10 residents have 5 relatives nearby, so 30 residents (20 + 10 = 30) have more than 3 relatives nearby.

12) The correct answer is D. Calculate the discount: $120 × 12.5% = $15 discount. Then subtract the discount from the original price to determine the sales price: $120 − $15 = $105

13) The correct answer is C. Divide by the fractional hour in order to determine the speed for an entire hour: 38.4 miles $\div \frac{4}{5}$ of an hour = 38.4 $\times \frac{5}{4}$ = (38 × 5) ÷ 4 = 48 mph

14) The correct answer is A. The ratio of defective chips to functioning chips is 1 to 20. So, the defective chips form one group and the functioning chips form another group. Therefore, the total data set can be divided into groups of 21. Accordingly, $\frac{1}{21}$ of the chips will be defective. The factory produced 11,235 chips last week, so we calculate as follows: 11,235 $\times \frac{1}{21}$ = 535

15) The correct answer is B. The total amount available is $55,000, so we can substitute this for C in the equation provided in order to calculate R number of residents:

C = $750R + $2,550

$55,000 = $750R + $2,550

$55,000 − $2,550 = $750R + $2,550 − $2,550

$55,000 − $2,550 = $750R

$52,450 = $750R

$52,450 ÷ $750 = $750R ÷ $750

$52,450 ÷ $750 = R

69.9 = R

It is not possible to accommodate a fractional part of one person, so we need to round down to 69 residents.

16) The correct answer is C. The value of μ must be greater than $^{11}/_3$, which is equal to 3.6667. The answer 4.1 is the only option which meets this criterion.

17) The correct answer is C. There are 2 stars for speeding, and each star equals 30 violations, so there were 60 speeding violations in total. The fine for speeding is $50 per violation, so the total amount collected for speeding violations was: 60 speeding violations × $50 per violation = $3000. There are three stars for other violations, which is equal to 90 violations (3 × 30 = 90). Other violations are $20 each, so the total for other violations is: 90 × $20 = $1800. Next, we need to deduct these two amounts from the total collections of $6,000 in order to find out how much was collected for parking violations: $6000 − $3000 − $1800 = $1200 in total for parking violations. There is one star for parking violations, so there were 30 parking violations. We divide to get the answer: $1200 income for parking violations ÷ 30 parking violations = $40 each

18) The correct answer is E. In order to solve this type of problem, you must do long division of the polynomial. Remember that you are subtracting the terms when you perform each part of the long division, so you need to be careful with negatives.

$$
\begin{array}{r}
x + 2 \\
x - 3 \overline{)\, x^2 - x - 6} \\
\underline{x^2 - 3x} \\
2x - 6 \\
\underline{2x - 6} \\
0
\end{array}
$$

19) The correct answer is B.

Step 1: Apply the distributive property of multiplication by multiplying the first term in the first set of parentheses by all of the terms inside the second pair of parentheses. Then multiply the second term from the first set of parentheses by all of the terms inside the second set of parentheses.

$(5ab - 6a)(3ab^3 - 4b^2 - 3a) =$
$(5ab × 3ab^3) + (5ab × -4b^2) + (5ab × -3a) + (-6a × 3ab^3) + (-6a × -4b^2) + (-6a × -3a)$

Step 2: Add up the individual products in order to solve the problem:
$(5ab × 3ab^3) + (5ab × -4b^2) + (5ab × -3a) + (-6a × 3ab^3) + (-6a × -4b^2) + (-6a × -3a) =$
$15a^2b^4 - 20ab^3 - 15a^2b - 18a^2b^3 + 24ab^2 + 18a^2$

20) The correct answer is a numerator value of 7 and a denominator value of 2.

Perform the multiplication on the terms in the parentheses first of all.
$4(2x + 2) = 6(x - 1) + 21$
$8x + 8 = (6x - 6) + 21$

Then move the terms with x so that they are on just one side of the equation.
$8x + 8 = 6x + 15$
$8x - 6x + 8 = 6x - 6x + 15$
$2x + 8 = 15$

Then deal with the integers.
$2x + 8 - 8 = 15 - 8$
$2x = 7$

Then express as a fraction to solve the problem.
$x = {}^7/_2$

21) The correct answer is E. The original price of the sofa on Wednesday was x. On Thursday, the sofa was reduced by 10%, so the price on Thursday was 90% of x or $0.90x$. On Friday, the sofa was reduced by a further 15%, so the price on Friday was 85% of the price on Thursday, so we can multiply Thursday's price by 0.85 to get our answer: $(0.90)(0.85)x$

22) The correct answer is E. The problem tells us that $2x + y = 6$ and $m - n = 2$, so we need to factor the problem into those terms first of all.
$(4x + 2y)(4m - 4n) =$
$2(2x + y) × 4(m - n)$
Then substitute the values provided into the equation.
$2(2x + y) × 4(m - n) =$
$2(6) × 4(2) =$
$(2 × 6) × (4 × 2) =$
$12 × 8 = 96$

23) The correct answer is B. Assign a variable for the age of each boy. Alex = A, Burt = B, and Zander = Z. Alex is twice as old as Burt, so A = 2B. Burt is one year older than three times the age of Zander, so B = 3Z + 1. Then substitute the value of B into the first equation.

121

A = 2B

A = 2(3Z + 1)

A = 6Z + 2

So, Alex is 2 years older than 6 times the age of Zander.

24) The correct answer is C. Remember that a fraction can also be expressed as division.

$$\frac{x+\frac{1}{5}}{\frac{1}{x}} = \left(x+\frac{1}{5}\right) \div \frac{1}{x}$$

In order to divide fractions, invert the second fraction and then multiply. To invert, swap the positions of the numerator and denominator in the second fraction. In this case $\frac{1}{x}$

becomes $\frac{x}{1}$ when inverted, which is then simplified to x.

$$\left(x+\frac{1}{5}\right) \div \frac{1}{x} =$$

$$\left(x+\frac{1}{5}\right) \times x =$$

$$x^2 + \frac{x}{5}$$

25) The correct answer is D. Get the integers to one side of the equation first of all.

$$\frac{1}{5}x + 3 = 5$$

$$\frac{1}{5}x + 3 - 3 = 5 - 3$$

$$\frac{1}{5}x = 2$$

Then multiply to eliminate the fraction and solve the problem.

$$\frac{1}{5}x \times 5 = 2 \times 5$$

$$x = 10$$

26) The correct answer is C. The first point on the graph lies at $x = 10$, so we can eliminate answer choices A and B. The point for the y coordinate that corresponds to $x = 10$ is 63 not 68, so we can eliminate answer choice D. The point for the y coordinate that corresponds to $x = 30$ is 49 not 42, so we can also eliminate answer choice E.

27) The correct answer is E. The first three bars of the graph represent the first 30 minutes, so add these three amounts together for your answer: 1.5 + 1.2 + 0.8 = 3.5 miles

28) The correct answer is D. Divide each side of the equation by 3. Then subtract 5 from both sides of the equation as shown below.
18 = 3(x + 5)
18 ÷ 3 = [3(x + 5)] ÷ 3
6 = x + 5
6 − 5 = x + 5 − 5
1 = x

29) The correct answer is B. Remember that factoring problems are just another type of equivalent expression question. Here, we have quite an advanced problem. Be sure to study the steps below carefully if you had trouble finding the solution for this problem.

For this type of problem, first you need to find the factors of the numerators and denominators of each fraction. When there are only addition signs in the rational expression, the factors will be in the following format: (+)(+)
If there is a negative sign, then the factors will be in this format: (+)(−)
You have to find the factors of the terms containing x or y variables, as well as the factors of the integers or other constants. It is usually best to start with finding the factors of the final integer in each polynomial expression.

Step 1: The numerator of the first fraction is $x^2 + 5x + 6$, so the final integer is 6.
The factors of 6 are:
1 × 6 = 6
2 × 3 = 6
Add these factors together to discover what integer you need to use in front of the second term of the expression.
1 + 6 = 7
2 + 3 = 5
2 and 3 satisfy both parts of the equation.
Therefore, the factors of $x^2 + 5x + 6$ are $(x + 2)(x + 3)$.

Step 2: Now factor the other parts of the problem. The denominator of the first fraction is $x^2 + 6x + 8$, so the final integer is 8.

The factors of 8 are:

1 × 8 = 8

2 × 4 = 8

Then add these factors together to find the integer to use in front of the second term of the expression.

1 + 8 = 9

2 + 4 = 6

Therefore, the factors of $x^2 + 6x + 8$ are $(x+2)(x+4)$.

Step 3: The numerator of the second fraction is $x^2 + 4x$, so there is no final integer. Because x is common to both terms of the expression, the factor will be in this format: $x(x + \ )$. Therefore, in order to factor $x^2 + 4x$, we express it as $x(x+4)$.

Step 4: The denominator of the second fraction is $x^2 + 8x + 15$, so the final integer is 15. The factors of 15 are:

1 × 15 = 15

3 × 5 = 15

Add these factors together to find the integer to use in front of the second term of the expression.

1 + 15 = 16

3 + 5 = 8

Therefore, the factors of $x^2 + 8x + 15$ are $(x+3)(x+5)$.

A good shortcut for this type of problem is to remind yourself that it is a problem about factoring, so the factors you find in step 1 will probably be common to other parts of the expression.

In other words, we discovered in step 1 that the factors of $x^2 + 5x + 6$ are $(x+2)$ and $(x+3)$.

So, when you are factoring out the other parts of the problem, start with $(x+2)$ and $(x+3)$.

Now that we have completed all of the four steps above, we can set out our problem with the factors we discovered in each step. We can see the factors of each fraction more clearly as show below.

$$\frac{x^2+5x+16}{x^2+6x+8}=\frac{(x+2)(x+3)}{(x+2)(x+4)} \qquad \frac{x^2+4x}{x^2+8x+15}=\frac{x(x+4)}{(x+3)(x+5)}$$

The problem should be set up as follows after you have found the factors:

$$\frac{x^2+5x+6}{x^2+6x+8}\times\frac{x^2+4x}{x^2+8x+15}=\frac{(x+2)(x+3)}{(x+2)(x+4)}\times\frac{x(x+4)}{(x+3)(x+5)}$$

Then you need to simplify by removing the common factors. Remove $(x + 2)$ from the first fraction.

$$\frac{(x+2)(x+3)}{(x+2)(x+4)}\times\frac{x(x+4)}{(x+3)(x+5)}=\frac{(x+3)}{(x+4)}\times\frac{x(x+4)}{(x+3)(x+5)}$$

Once you have simplified each fraction as much as possible, perform the operation indicated. In this problem, we are multiplying. So, we can express the two factored-out fractions as one fraction and then remove the other common terms.

$$\frac{(x+3)}{(x+4)}\times\frac{x(x+4)}{(x+3)(x+5)}=\frac{(x+3)(x+4)x}{(x+4)(x+3)(x+5)}$$

You can remove $(x + 3)$ from the above fraction since it is in both the numerator and denominator.

$$\frac{(x+3)(x+4)x}{(x+4)(x+3)(x+5)}=\frac{(x+4)x}{(x+4)(x+5)}$$

We can further simplify by removing $(x +4)$.

$$\frac{(x+4)x}{(x+4)(x+5)}=\frac{x}{(x+5)}$$

So, our final answer is $\dfrac{x}{x+5}$

30) The correct answer is C. If the amount earned from selling jackets was one-third that of selling jeans, the ratio of jacket to jean sales was 1 to 3. So, we need to divide the total sales of $4,000 into $1,000 for jackets and $3,000 for jeans. We can then solve as follows: $3,000 in jeans sales ÷ $20 per pair = 150 pairs sold

31) The correct answer is A. The special operation is defined as $(x \text{ Д } y) = (5x \div 4y)$. Looking at the relationship between the left-hand side and the right-hand side of this equation, we can determine the operations that need to be performed on any new equation containing the operation Д and variables x and y. For our problem, the new equation will be carried out as follows: Operation Д is division $(5x \div 4y)$; the number or variable immediately after the opening parenthesis is multiplied by 5 (**5**$x \div 4y$); the number or variable immediately before the closing parenthesis is multiplied by 4 $(5x \div \mathbf{4}y)$. So, the new equation $(8 \text{ Д } y) = 5$ becomes $(5 \times 8) \div (4 \times y) = 5$.

Now solve for y:

(5 × 8) ÷ (4 × y) = 5

40 ÷ 4y = 5

40 ÷ 4y × 4y = 5 × 4y

40 = 5 × 4y

40 = 20y

40 ÷ 20 = 20y ÷ 20

y = 2

32) The correct answer is A. For algebraic equivalency questions like this, you can perform the operations on each of the answer choices to see which one is equivalent. Remember to be careful when performing multiplication on negative numbers inside parentheticals.

6 + 2(15 − x) =

6 + (2 × 15) + (2 × −x) =

6 + 30 − 2x =

36 − 2x

33) The correct answer is B. The total of the monthly payments is:

$700 per month × 360 months = $252,000

The total price of the house is $300,000 so deduct the total payments from this amount in order to calculate the immediate payment: $300,000 − $252,000 = $48,000

34) The correct answer is A. To divide, invert the second fraction and then multiply as shown.

$$\frac{x}{5} \div \frac{9}{y} = \frac{x}{5} \times \frac{y}{9} = \frac{x \times y}{5 \times 9} = \frac{xy}{45}$$

35) The correct answers are D and E. The formula for the area of a circle is: πR^2. The area of circle A is $\pi \times 5^2 = 25\pi$ and the area of circle B is $\pi \times 3^2 = 9\pi$. So, the difference between the areas is 16π.

The formula for circumference is: $\pi 2R$. The circumference of circle A is $\pi \times 2 \times 5 = 10\pi$ and the circumference for circle B is $\pi \times 2 \times 3 = 6\pi$. The difference in the circumferences is 4π. So, answer D is correct.

Diameter is equal to the radius times 2, so the diameter of circle A is 10 and the diameter of circle B is 6, and the difference in diameters is 4. So, answer E is also correct.

36) The correct answer is C. Calculate the area for each of the cupboards: 8 × 2 = 16 and 5 × 2 = 10. Therefore, the total area for both cupboards is 16 + 10 = 26. Then find the area for the entire kitchen: 8 × 12 = 96. Then deduct the cupboards from the total: 96 − 26 = 70

37) The correct answer is B. Circumference is $2\pi R$, so the circumference of the large wheel is 20π and the circumference of the smaller wheel is 12π. If the large wheel travels 360 revolutions, it travels a distance of: $20\pi \times 360 = 7200\pi$. To determine the number of revolutions the small wheel needs to make to go the same distance, we divide the distance by the circumference of the smaller wheel: $7200\pi \div 12\pi = 600$. Finally, calculate the difference in the number of revolutions: $600 - 360 = 240$

38) The correct answer is A. For questions like this on arcs, you should first find the circumference of the circle. The diameter of the circle is 2, so the circumference is 2π. There are 360 degrees in a circle and the question is asking us about a 90 degree angle, so the arc length relates to one-fourth of the circumference: $90 \div 360 = {}^{1}/_{4}$. So, we need to take one-fourth of the circumference to get the answer: $2\pi \times {}^{1}/_{4} = {}^{2\pi}/_{4} = {}^{\pi}/_{2}$

39) The correct answer is B. The two sides of the field form a right angle, so we can use the Pythagorean theorem to solve the problem: $\sqrt{3^2 + 4^2} = \sqrt{9 + 16} = \sqrt{25} = 5$

40) The correct answer is A. First, we need to find the circumference of the semicircle on the left side of the figure. The width of the rectangle of 10 inches forms the diameter of the semicircle, so the circumference of an entire circle with a diameter of 10 inches would be 10π inches. We need the circumference for a semicircle only, which is half of a circle, so we need to divide the circumference by 2: $10\pi \div 2 = 5\pi$. Since the right side of the figure is an equilateral triangle, the two sides of the triangle have the same length as the width of the rectangle, so they are 10 inches each. Finally, you need to add up the lengths of all of the sides to get the answer: $18 + 18 + 10 + 10 + 5\pi = 56 + 5\pi$ inches

41) The correct answer is D. To solve the problem, insert the values provided in the problem into the formula for the volume of a pyramid: $\frac{1}{3} \times$ length × width × height

$\frac{1}{3} \times$ length × width × height = 30

$\frac{1}{3} \times 5 \times 3 \times$ height = 30

$\frac{15}{3} \times$ height = 30

5 × height = 30

5 ÷ 5 × height = 30 ÷ 5

height = 6

42) The correct answer is A. Since the left and right sides of this figure are not parallel, the figure is classified as a trapezoid. To find the area of a trapezoid we take the average of the length of the top (T) and bottom (B) and multiply by the height (H):

$$\frac{T+B}{2} \times H =$$

$$\frac{7+12}{2} \times 6 =$$

$$9.5 \times 6 = 57$$

43) The correct answer is a numerator value of 1 and a denominator value of 4. Calculate the area of the triangle: $\frac{1}{2} \times base \times height = \frac{1}{2} \times 5 \times 6 = \frac{1}{2} \times 30 = 15$. The height of the unshaded part is 9 inches since $15 - 6 = 9$, so next we can calculate the area of the unshaded rectangular part: $base \times height = 5 \times 9 = 45$. Add the area of the unshaded part of the figure to the area of the triangle in order to get the area for the entire figure: $45 + 15 = 60$. Finally, express the result as a simplified fraction with the area of the triangle in the numerator and the area of the entire figure in the denominator: $^{15}/_{60} = {}^{1}/_{4}$

44) The correct answers are $\sqrt{34}$ and 4. Here we have a right triangle with three sides, the measurements of which are 3, 5, and an unknown length that we will call x. We do not know which of the lengths represents the hypotenuse, so we have to use the Pythagorean theorem for three scenarios:

<u>Hypotenuse = x</u>
$$\sqrt{3^2 + 5^2} = x$$
$$\sqrt{9 + 25} = x$$
$$\sqrt{34} = x$$

<u>Hypotenuse = 5</u>
$$\sqrt{3^2 + x^2} = 5$$
$$\sqrt{9 + x^2} = 5$$
Then square both sides of the equation to eliminate the radical.
$$(\sqrt{9 + x^2})^2 = 5^2$$
$$9 + x^2 = 25$$
$$x^2 = 25 - 9$$
$$x^2 = 16$$
$$x = 4$$

<u>Hypotenuse = 3</u>

$\sqrt{5^2 + x^2} = 3$

$\sqrt{25 + x^2} = 3$

Then square both sides of the equation to eliminate the radical.

$(\sqrt{25 + x^2})^2 = 9$

$25 + x^2 = 9$

$x^2 = 9 - 25$

$x^2 = -16$

Real number square roots do not exist for negative numbers, so the hypotenuse cannot have a length of 3 in this problem.

45) The correct answers are B and C. When a transversal crosses two parallel lines, opposite angles will be equal in measure and corresponding angles will also be equal in measure. (Corresponding angles are angles in the matching same-shaped corners.) Angles $\angle$b and $\angle$c are opposite angles and angles $\angle$c and $\angle$f are corresponding angles, so answer B is correct. Angles $\angle$b and $\angle$e are corresponding and angles $\angle$e and $\angle$f are opposite, so answer C is also correct.

46) The correct answer is B. Our data set is: 2.5, 9.4, 3.1, 1.7, 3.2, 8.2, 4.5, 6.4, 7.8. First, put the numbers in ascending order: 1.7, 2.5, 3.1, 3.2, 4.5, 6.4, 7.8, 8.2, 9.4. The median is the number in the middle of the set: 1.7, 2.5, 3.1, 3.2, **4.5**, 6.4, 7.8, 8.2, 9.4

47) The correct answer is A. The outcome of an earlier roll does not affect the outcome of the next roll. When rolling a pair of dice, the possibility of an odd number is always $1/2$, just as the possibility of an even number is always $1/2$. We can prove this mathematically by looking at the possible outcomes:

1,1 1,2 1,3 1,4 1,5 1,6
2,1 2,2 2,3 2,4 2,5 2,6
3,1 3,2 3,3 3,4 3,5 3,6
4,1 4,2 4,3 4,4 4,5 4,6
5,1 5,2 5,3 5,4 5,5 5,6
6,1 6,2 6,3 6,4 6,5 6,6

The odd number combinations are highlighted:

1,1 **1,2** 1,3 **1,4** 1,5 **1,6**
2,1 2,2 **2,3** 2,4 **2,5** 2,6
3,1 **3,2** 3,3 **3,4** 3,5 **3,6**
4,1 4,2 **4,3** 4,4 **4,5** 4,6
5,1 **5,2** 5,3 **5,4** 5,5 **5,6**
6,1 6,2 **6,3** 6,4 **6,5** 6,6

So, we can see that an odd number will be rolled half of the time.

48) The correct answer is E. The proposed course of action affects the residents of Buford, so the statistical sample must represent these residents as much as possible. The most representative sample would therefore be achieved by selecting participants for a survey from a list of all of the citizens living in Buford. Answers A and B may represent people living in other areas who are merely driving near Buford. Answers C and D would fail to represent residents of Buford who do not drive or who have not registered to vote.

49) The correct answer is D. To find the mean, add up all of the items in the set and then divide by the number of items in the set. Here we have 7 numbers in the set, so we get our answer as follows: $(89 + 65 + 75 + 68 + 82 + 74 + 86) \div 7 = 539 \div 7 = 77$

50) The correct answer is B. At the start of the party, there are 10 red balloons, 7 green balloons, 6 purple balloons, 5 orange balloons, and 11 blue balloons in the bag, so we add all of these up to get our data set at the beginning: $10 + 7 + 6 + 5 + 11 = 39$ items in the data set at the beginning. Then a blue balloon and an orange balloon are removed, so we need to reduce the data set for these two items: $39 - 2 = 37$. The problem is asking about the probability of a blue balloon. There are 11 blue balloons at the start and one has been removed, so there are 10 blue balloons left. Remember to express the probability as a fraction with the possibility of the outcome in the numerator and the remaining data set in the denominator: $^{10}/_{37}$

51) The correct answer is E. We have the data set: 1.6, 2.9, 4.5, 2.5, 2.5, 5.1, 5.4 The mode is the number that occurs most frequently. 2.5 occurs twice, but the other numbers only occur once. So, 2.5 is the mode.

52) The correct answer is A. For line (A) the mean is $(2 + 3 + 3 + 3 + 4) \div 5 = 3$, and the median is also 3 because it is the number that in halfway in the data set: 2, 3, **3**, 3, 4.

53) The correct answer is B. We don't know the age of the 10th car, so put this in as x to solve: $(2 + 3 + 4 + 5 + 6 + 7 + 9 + 10 + 12 + x) \div 10 = 6$
$[(2 + 3 + 4 + 5 + 6 + 7 + 9 + 10 + 12 + x) \div 10] \times 10 = 6 \times 10$
$2 + 3 + 4 + 5 + 6 + 7 + 9 + 10 + 12 + x = 60$
$58 + x = 60$
$x = 2$

54) The correct answers are (2) and (5). Statistical questions ask about behaviors or opinions. So, the following are statistical questions: "How many residents of the town oppose the tax increase?" and "Do most college graduates in our state find jobs within one year of leaving college?"

55) The correct answers are A and B. The range is the difference between the highest number and the lowest number in a data set. If the range increases by 2, then the

highest number could go up by 2 or the highest and lowest numbers could increase and decrease by 1 each respectively.

56) The correct answer is E. We have 54 cards in the deck (13 × 4 = 52). We have taken out two spades, one heart, and a club, thereby removing 4 cards. So, the available data set is 48 (52 − 4 = 48). The desired outcome is drawing a heart. We have 13 hearts to begin with and one has been removed, so there are 12 hearts left. So, the probability of drawing a heart is $^{12}/_{48} = {}^{1}/_{4}$

CPSIA information can be obtained
at www.ICGtesting.com
Printed in the USA
BVHW011256180319
542969BV00009B/93/P